HOPE ANDRUS

SOMATIC THERAPY

FOR TRAUMA RECOVERY

TOOLKIT OF EXERCISES FOR STRENGTHENING THE MIND-BODY CONNECTION, TREATING COMPLEX TRAUMA, RELIEVE STRESS, AND PTSD.

SOMATIC THERAPY

FOR

TRAUMA RECOVERY

Toolkit of Exercises for Strengthening the Mind-Body Connection, Treating Complex Trauma, Relieve Stress, and PTSD.

DR. HOPE ANDRUS

Editorial Director:

Tom Jones

Cover Design:

James Griffith

Editorial and Production Services:

True Pen Publishers

Contents

Preface

Welcome to a journey of healing, where the power of your body and mind can guide you toward peace, resilience, and a renewed sense of self. If you're holding this book, you've already taken an important step—acknowledging that your past doesn't have to define your future. Whether you're a survivor of childhood abuse or simply someone who has experienced trauma in any form, I want you to know that your story matters. You are not broken, and your path to healing is entirely your own. This book is here to offer guidance, encouragement, and practical tools, all rooted in the transformative practice of somatic therapy.

Somatic therapy, in its essence, is about reconnecting with your body. Trauma has a way of pulling us out of our own skin, making us feel disconnected from the very vessel that holds our experiences. It's as if our bodies betray us by holding onto pain, memories, and fear. But what if I told you that your body is not your enemy? In fact, it's your greatest ally in this journey. Through somatic practices, you'll learn to listen to your body's wisdom—its subtle signals, its calls for attention—and in doing so, you will unlock your innate ability to heal from within. This is not a process that happens overnight, nor is it one that will ever be perfect. But it is a process, and it's one that begins with the simple act of noticing, feeling, and allowing yourself the space to heal.

This book is designed to be your companion in this exploration. It's not a rigid manual filled with technical jargon, but rather a guide that meets you where you are—whether you're just beginning to explore the impact of trauma on your life, or you're looking for new ways to deepen your healing. We'll dive into practical techniques like grounding, mindful movement, and breathing exercises that help you stay present when the weight of the past feels too heavy to carry. We'll explore how your body reacts to stress and trauma, and more importantly, how you can retrain it to feel safe again. As you turn the pages, you'll discover stories of resilience, moments of breakthrough, and insights that remind you: healing is not only possible, it's within your reach.

As you read, think of this book as a conversation between us. I'm not here to tell you what to do or how to feel. I'm here to offer suggestions, to share what has worked for others, and to remind you that there is no one right way to heal. Every person's journey is different, shaped by individual experiences, challenges, and strengths. Some days will feel lighter, and others may feel like you're carrying the weight of the world on your shoulders. But that's okay. Healing isn't a race; it's a slow, steady reclamation of yourself.

Trauma can often feel like a storm that sweeps through your life, leaving chaos and confusion in its wake. But even after the darkest storms, there is always a clearing. There is always a moment when the clouds part, and you begin to see the sun filtering through again. This book is about finding that clearing, about reclaiming your sense of peace and power, no matter how distant they may feel. You don't have to rush or force anything. In fact, the beauty of somatic therapy is that it teaches you to be patient with yourself, to trust your body's own pace, and to recognize that healing is as much about the journey as it is about the destination.

I invite you to move through these pages with a sense of curiosity. Be open to the exercises, even if they seem unfamiliar at first. Pay attention to what resonates with you and what doesn't—that's all part of the process. Some days, just reading a single paragraph might feel like enough. Other days, you might find yourself eagerly diving into the techniques and exercises, wanting to try them all at once. Whatever pace feels right for you is the right pace. This is your time, your space, your healing.

As we begin this journey together, I want you to know that you are not alone. Countless others have walked this path before you, and while your story is uniquely yours, the hope and healing you seek are shared by many. Together, we will explore the ways in which you can reconnect with yourself, reclaim your inner strength, and move forward with a renewed sense of hope and possibility. Let this book be your guide, your companion, and your reminder that you are capable of not only surviving but thriving. Healing from trauma is not easy, but it is absolutely possible. You have everything you need within you, and I'm honored to walk alongside you as you discover that truth for yourself.

Introduction

Welcome to Your Healing Journey

Trauma is an experience that overwhelms the mind, body, and emotions, leaving you feeling helpless, unsafe, and disconnected. It can be caused by a wide range of events, from physical abuse and emotional neglect to accidents or the sudden loss of a loved one. Trauma doesn't just come from extreme events like war or natural disasters; even experiences that seem small to others can have a profound impact. What matters is how the event made you feel—whether it left you overwhelmed, scared, or powerless. In its simplest form, trauma is anything that the mind and body perceive as too much to handle.

When trauma occurs, it doesn't just stay in your mind as a distant memory. It lives in your body, shaping the way you think, feel, and physically respond to the world around you. Trauma affects the brain in profound ways, particularly the areas responsible for processing fear, memory, and emotion. The part of your brain known as the amygdala, often called the brain's "alarm system," becomes hyperactive when you experience trauma. It goes into overdrive, constantly scanning your environment for danger, even when no real threat is present. This is why many trauma survivors feel on edge or anxious, as if something bad could happen at any moment.

At the same time, the prefrontal cortex, which helps you make rational decisions and calm your emotions, struggles to function properly. This is why it can feel nearly impossible to "talk yourself out" of fear or panic after a traumatic experience. The rational part of your brain isn't fully in control—your survival instincts are. Meanwhile, the hippocampus, which helps to organize and store memories, can also become disrupted. This is why trauma often leaves you with fragmented or disjointed memories, where certain details are clear, but the overall event feels foggy or disoriented.

Trauma doesn't just impact your brain; it deeply affects your nervous system as well. The nervous system has two primary states—fight-or-flight, which prepares you to face or escape danger, and rest-and-digest, which allows you to relax and recover. When you experience trauma, your body often becomes stuck in the fight-or-flight mode, unable to fully return to a state of calm. Even when the immediate danger has passed, your body remains on high alert. This can lead to a range of symptoms, including chronic anxiety, difficulty sleeping, or feeling jumpy and easily startled. Over time, this constant state of stress can wear down your body, leading to exhaustion and burnout.

For many people, trauma manifests as chronic stress that affects both their mental and physical health. This is because trauma isn't just something that happens in the past; it lingers in the body, tightening muscles, speeding up your heart rate, and creating a sense of unease. You might notice tension in your shoulders, neck, or back that just won't go away, or experience headaches, stomach issues, or chest pain without any clear medical cause. These physical symptoms are your body's way of expressing the unresolved trauma stored within. It's as if your body is still carrying the weight of the experience, even if your mind is trying to move on.

The mind-body connection becomes especially clear when you consider how unresolved trauma can fuel anxiety. Anxiety is essentially your brain and body being stuck in a loop of fear and hypervigilance. After trauma, your nervous system is constantly bracing for the worst, even if there's no immediate threat. This ongoing anxiety can leave you feeling drained and disconnected from yourself and others. You might feel like you're always one step away from falling apart, or like your body is revving its engine even when you're standing still.

Physical pain is another common manifestation of trauma. This can be because your body, in response to trauma, holds onto tension as a form of protection.

Muscles stay tight, joints may feel stiff, and you might develop chronic pain conditions like fibromyalgia or other stress-related ailments. The body is incredibly resilient, but when it's constantly under stress, it begins to wear down. The body's natural systems—like digestion, immune function, and sleep—can all be disrupted, leaving you feeling fatigued, sick, or run-down.

What makes trauma especially complex is that it isn't always obvious to the person experiencing it. Many people go through life thinking that feeling anxious, stressed, or physically uncomfortable is just "normal." They might not connect these feelings to a traumatic experience from their past. But whether the trauma is big or small, it leaves its mark. And until it's addressed, it can continue to affect your body and mind in ways that seem unrelated, such as chronic illness, mood swings, or trouble focusing.

Healing from trauma requires understanding how deeply it affects both the mind and the body. You can't simply think your way out of it or will yourself to feel better. Trauma has to be worked through on a physical level, using techniques that help you reconnect with your body and re-establish a sense of safety within. Only then can the nervous system begin to calm, and the brain can start to rewire itself away from fear and toward healing.

Why Somatic Therapy Works: Healing Through the Body

Somatic therapy is built on the understanding that trauma doesn't just live in our minds—it lives in our bodies. When we experience something traumatic, especially over an extended period or during vulnerable stages of life, our body goes into survival mode. The body's natural response to danger is the fight, flight, or freeze reaction. This is an instinctive, automatic process that floods the system with stress hormones like adrenaline and cortisol, preparing us to respond to the perceived threat. In the moment of trauma, these responses can save our lives. However, when the body is overwhelmed and unable to fully process the traumatic event, it stores the physical and emotional impact of that experience within itself. That's where somatic therapy comes in: it uses the body as the gateway to release this stored trauma and help us heal from within.

At its core, somatic therapy recognizes that the body remembers. Even when our conscious mind tries to forget or move on, the body holds onto the trauma in ways that can manifest as chronic tension, anxiety, and other symptoms of post-traumatic stress disorder (PTSD). This can happen without us even realizing it. You might feel a knot in your stomach when something reminds you of a past event, or your shoulders might tighten up during moments of stress, and yet the connection between those physical sensations and your past trauma may not be immediately clear. The body is often working silently in the background, trying to protect you by holding onto those memories and emotions, even when they are no longer helpful.

The science behind somatic therapy is deeply rooted in how the nervous system operates. Trauma disrupts the natural balance of the autonomic nervous system, which regulates many of our body's essential functions, including heart rate, digestion, and the stress response. In particular, trauma often leaves us stuck in a state of heightened arousal, known as hypervigilance, or in a state of shutdown, where we feel disconnected and numb. Somatic therapy works by helping to restore balance to this system. Through gentle movement, breathing exercises, and body awareness techniques, it creates an opportunity for the nervous system to regulate itself. These practices help bring the body out of a constant state of "fight or flight" and into a place where healing can occur.

For instance, one of the most powerful tools in somatic therapy is grounding. Grounding involves bringing attention to the present moment by focusing on physical sensations in the body. This could be as simple as feeling your feet firmly planted on the ground or noticing the sensation of your breath moving in and out of your lungs. These techniques might seem basic, but they are incredibly effective at calming the nervous system. When we are grounded, our body starts to shift out of the fight-or-flight state and back into what is called the "rest and digest" state, where true healing can happen. Grounding helps remind the body that, in this moment, it is safe.

Another key aspect of somatic therapy is releasing the tension and energy that the body has held onto since the trauma occurred. In moments of trauma, the body often braces itself, muscles tighten, and energy builds up in the system, preparing for action. But if that energy doesn't get discharged—because we were unable to run, fight, or otherwise respond—our body keeps holding onto it. Somatic techniques, such as mindful movement or shaking, help release this trapped energy in a safe, controlled way. For example, a somatic therapist might guide you through a gentle shaking exercise, which mimics the body's natural response to stress release, helping you discharge the energy that's been stored since the trauma. This not only helps calm the nervous system but also allows the body to complete the process it began during the traumatic event.

Somatic therapy also focuses on the importance of body awareness. Trauma can make us feel disconnected from our bodies, as if we are floating above ourselves or stuck in a fog. This dissociation is a natural protective mechanism when the pain feels too much to bear, but it also makes it difficult to fully heal. Through somatic therapy, you're encouraged to tune back into your body in small, manageable ways. Maybe you start by simply noticing how your body feels when you're lying down or sitting. Over time, as you become more comfortable with your body's signals, you can begin to explore deeper sensations and emotions. This reconnection allows you to develop a sense of safety in your own body, which is crucial for healing from trauma.

One of the most important aspects of somatic therapy is that it moves at the body's pace. Trauma survivors often feel pressured to "get over it" or move forward, but somatic therapy doesn't rush the process. It recognizes that healing takes time and that the body knows when it's ready to release the trauma. By working with the body rather than against it, somatic therapy creates a safe, nurturing environment where deep healing can occur. The process may involve releasing stored tension, expressing emotions that have been held in for too long, or simply allowing yourself to feel grounded and present for the first time in a long while.

In essence, somatic therapy helps the body reclaim its natural balance. It provides tools that calm the nervous system, reduce the symptoms of PTSD, stress, and anxiety, and offer a way to process the trauma that the mind alone may not be able to reach. By focusing on the body's innate wisdom and its ability to heal, somatic therapy offers a pathway to recovery that feels both gentle and empowering.

Your Healing Journey Starts Here: A Compassionate Approach

Healing from trauma is a deeply personal journey, and I want to invite you to approach it with the gentleness and compassion you deserve. As you move through the chapters of this book, know that you are taking powerful steps toward reclaiming a sense of peace, safety, and control over your own body. The road ahead may seem daunting at times, but I want you to remember this: you are not defined by your trauma, and the path to healing is not something you have to walk alone.

Somatic therapy offers a unique and empowering way to reconnect with yourself, especially after experiencing the disconnection that trauma so often brings. Trauma can make us feel like our bodies are no longer safe places to be, as if the very vessel that holds us has been compromised. But through somatic practices, we learn that the body is not just a witness to pain—it is also the key to healing. Somatic therapy gently guides you back to yourself, helping you understand that your body holds the power to heal, to restore, and to protect you.

One of the most important things I want you to take away from this journey is the necessity of self-compassion. Healing doesn't happen all at once, and it certainly doesn't follow a straight line. There will be days when you feel like you're making great strides, and others when old memories or sensations might feel overwhelming. That's okay. It's all part of the process. Somatic therapy encourages you to honor where you are at any given moment—to listen to your body, to be present with it, and to allow whatever feelings arise without judgment. Think of it as a conversation between you and your body, where you finally give yourself permission to feel and respond to what has been buried for so long.

It's important to be patient with yourself, too. Trauma recovery, especially through somatic methods, is not a quick fix. It's a gradual unravelling of the tension and fear that have taken root within you, and it requires a willingness to move at your own pace. There is no rush, and there is certainly no pressure to "get it right." In fact, one of the most profound lessons of somatic therapy is that healing happens in the small, subtle moments when you start to feel just a little bit safer in your body. Each breath, each movement, each mindful practice adds a layer of safety and trust back into your experience of yourself.

What makes somatic therapy so powerful is that it gives you tools to navigate the unpredictable waves of trauma. When flashbacks, anxiety, or stress threaten to take over, somatic techniques like grounding, breathing, and mindful movement help you find your footing. They teach you how to be present, how to self-soothe, and how to regain control when things feel chaotic. The beauty of these practices is that they are always available to you—whether you're in the midst of a stressful situation or reflecting quietly on your own. They help anchor you in the here and now, reminding you that even though your past may have shaped you, it does not have to define you.

As you begin to explore these techniques, I encourage you to stay open to the idea of possibility. The body's capacity to heal is incredible, even after trauma has altered how you feel within it. Through somatic therapy, many people have regained a sense of peace and safety they once thought was lost forever. You may discover moments of calm where there once was fear, or a sense of empowerment where there once was helplessness. These are the victories that matter most. And they come not from forcing yourself to heal, but from gently allowing yourself to feel safe again, one step at a time.

Every practice you engage with, whether it's breathing deeply through a tough moment or tuning into your body's needs after a stressful day, is a step toward restoring your relationship with yourself. Over time, these small practices begin to accumulate. Little by little, they help you reclaim control over your own body and your life, making room for the possibility of peace. The more you engage with these techniques, the more you'll notice that the intense grip trauma once had over you starts to loosen. The sensations that once triggered fear and panic will gradually become easier to manage, and in time, you'll feel a growing sense of calm.

Remember that healing is not about erasing your past— it's about building a future where you can feel whole again. With patience, self-compassion, and the powerful tools offered by somatic therapy, you'll find that this future is not only possible but entirely within your reach. Let this book be your guide, but more importantly, trust that your body knows the way forward.

Chapter 1

Trauma and the Body – What You Need to Know

Trauma doesn't just affect the mind; it leaves its mark on the body as well, often in ways we don't fully understand until we stop and listen. Our bodies are intricate storytellers, holding onto the experiences and emotions that we've been through, whether we're aware of it or not. When we think of trauma, we often picture the emotional pain it brings—fear, anxiety, sadness. But trauma also resides deeply in our muscles, organs, and nervous system, manifesting in a range of physical and emotional signs that can linger long after the traumatic event has passed. These signs are not random; they're the body's way of trying to cope with, protect itself from, and make sense of the distress it has endured.

One of the most common ways trauma shows up in the body is through chronic pain. Whether it's persistent back pain, tension headaches, or unexplained aches, these symptoms often have roots in unresolved trauma. Think of how the body naturally responds to fear—your muscles tighten, your shoulders hunch, your jaw clenches. Over time, if the body remains in this state of high alert, these physical reactions can become ingrained. Muscle tension may become a constant companion, locking the body into patterns of tightness and discomfort. Trauma can also disrupt the body's natural rhythms, leading to digestive issues like irritable bowel syndrome or chronic stomach discomfort, as the gut—the body's "second brain"—is highly sensitive to emotional stress.

Fatigue is another sign that trauma is still being held in the body. Living in a state of prolonged stress wears down your energy reserves. The body, caught in a continuous fight-or-flight mode, becomes exhausted from being constantly on edge. This kind of fatigue goes beyond needing a good night's sleep; it's a deep, bone-weary exhaustion that comes from the body being in survival mode for too long. It's as if your entire system is saying, "I can't keep running from this anymore."

Emotionally, trauma can manifest in several ways. Hypervigilance is one of the most telling signs. When you've experienced trauma, your nervous system remains on high alert, scanning for danger even when there's none present. This can feel like you're always bracing for something bad to happen, making it difficult to relax or feel safe. You might find yourself startled by loud noises, overly sensitive to your environment, or constantly checking over your shoulder. This heightened state of awareness is your body's way of protecting you, but over time, it becomes exhausting and disconnects you from the present moment.

Dissociation is another way the body copes with trauma. It's a protective mechanism, almost like your mind leaving your body for a while because the present moment feels too unbearable to face. When someone dissociates, they may feel disconnected from their surroundings or as if they're watching themselves from the outside. This feeling of being detached from reality or from one's own emotions is the body's way of numbing out overwhelming pain. It's a survival technique, but like all trauma responses, it's not sustainable and can leave you feeling disoriented and alienated from yourself.

Emotional numbness often accompanies dissociation. After trauma, you might find that you can't feel joy, sadness, or any strong emotions at all. It's as if your emotional volume has been turned all the way down to prevent further pain. While this might seem like a relief at first, over time, it can leave you feeling disconnected not only from the difficult emotions but from the positive ones as well. This emotional flatness is the body's way of trying to protect you from further harm, but it can make life feel dull and unfulfilling.

All these symptoms—whether physical or emotional—are the body's way of holding onto past trauma. Trauma leaves a mark because it's an overwhelming experience that the body wasn't prepared to process at the time it happened. So, instead of moving through the experience, the body holds onto it. The muscles store tension, the nervous system stays on alert, and the emotional centers of the brain either heighten or shut down completely. It's like the trauma is frozen inside you, waiting to be thawed. And until it's released, these physical and emotional signs persist, reminding you of a past you may wish to leave behind but that your body is still carrying.

This is why somatic therapy is so crucial in trauma recovery. It addresses these deeply held experiences not by simply talking about them but by working directly with the body, the very place where the trauma resides. Understanding that these symptoms are not random or "all in your head" is the first step toward healing. Your body is trying to communicate with you, and through gentle, compassionate somatic practices, you can begin to listen, release, and ultimately reclaim a sense of peace in both your body and mind.

Understanding the Nervous System: Fight, Flight, Freeze

When we encounter a traumatic event, our body's natural response is to activate the nervous system in a way that prepares us to survive. This is often referred to as the fight, flight, or freeze response, a set of instinctual behaviors designed to protect us in moments of danger. Imagine yourself in a situation where you feel threatened—your heart races, your breath quickens, and your muscles tense. These physiological changes are part of a deeply embedded survival mechanism that has evolved over millennia.

Let's break down these responses a bit more. The fight response is our body's way of gearing up to confront the threat head-on. It's an assertive, powerful reaction where we might feel a surge of adrenaline, giving us strength and energy to either defend ourselves or take charge of the situation. In contrast, the flight response prepares us to escape or flee from danger. It triggers a rush of energy that enables us to run faster, move quickly, and get away from perceived harm. Lastly, there's the freeze response, which can sometimes feel like a paradox in the heat of the moment. In this state, the body essentially immobilizes itself. It's as if we've hit a pause button, often a last resort when fight or flight doesn't seem viable. This can be particularly poignant in situations where individuals feel utterly helpless, such as in cases of abuse or overwhelming fear.

These responses can be incredibly effective in the short term, allowing us to react swiftly to danger and survive traumatic encounters. However, the challenge arises when these survival mechanisms become stuck in the body. After the immediate threat has passed, our nervous system can sometimes remain in a heightened state of alert. This is particularly common in individuals who have experienced trauma. The body, having gone through a period of extreme stress, may find it difficult to reset and return to a state of calm. Instead, it holds onto the remnants of the trauma, causing ongoing stress and anxiety.

Imagine your nervous system as a finely tuned instrument. When trauma strikes, it can feel like that instrument is strummed out of tune, and the echoes of that dissonance linger long after the event. As a result, everyday situations can provoke reactions that seem out of proportion, leaving individuals feeling as though they're still in danger even when they are safe. This can manifest as heightened sensitivity to stress, chronic anxiety, or an ever-present sense of unease that colors daily life.

It's also worth noting that the freeze response can lead to feelings of disconnection or numbness, making it hard for individuals to fully engage with their emotions or surroundings. Many find themselves stuck in a loop, oscillating between hyperarousal (where they are overly alert and reactive) and dissociation (where they feel disconnected from their bodies or reality). This fluctuation can create a challenging cycle, trapping them in a state of survival mode long after the immediate threat has subsided.

Understanding these responses and their effects on the body is crucial for anyone on the path to recovery. It illuminates why certain triggers can provoke intense reactions and helps us recognize that these feelings, while uncomfortable, are valid responses to our experiences. Healing becomes about learning to navigate this complex landscape of emotions and sensations, finding ways to gently guide the nervous system back to a place of balance and calm. With the right tools and practices, we can begin to release these stuck responses, paving the way for a more peaceful and empowered existence.

How Somatic Therapy Helps Release Stored Trauma

Somatic therapy operates on the understanding that trauma is not merely a psychological phenomenon; it is deeply embedded in our bodies. When we experience trauma, whether it's a single event or a series of distressing experiences, our bodies respond instinctively. This can manifest as a rush of adrenaline, increased heart rate, or the feeling of being frozen in place. These physical responses are essential for survival, but when the threat has passed, the residual energy often remains trapped within our muscles, tissues, and nervous systems. This unprocessed energy can lead to a range of issues, from chronic pain and tension to anxiety and depression. Thus, addressing trauma requires more than just talk therapy; it demands a holistic approach that honors the body's role in the healing process.

At its core, somatic therapy encourages us to listen to our bodies and recognize the messages they send. It invites us to explore physical sensations—those tight knots in our stomachs or the heaviness in our chests—as gateways to understanding our emotional experiences. One of the primary methods of releasing this stored trauma is through gentle, mindful movement. Simple exercises like shaking or dancing can facilitate the natural release of pent-up energy. Imagine standing in a comfortable space, allowing your body to move freely, maybe even letting your arms and legs shake out as if you were a rag doll. This unstructured movement can help you access feelings and sensations that have long been buried, fostering a sense of liberation and lightness.

Breathwork is another cornerstone of somatic practice that can profoundly impact the way we process trauma. Our breath is intimately connected to our emotional state; when we're stressed or anxious, our breathing tends to become shallow and rapid. In contrast, deep, intentional breathing can help ground us, allowing for the release of stored tension. A simple exercise to try is the "4-7-8 breath": inhale deeply for a count of four, hold that breath for seven counts, and then exhale slowly for eight counts. This rhythmic breathing not only calms the nervous system but also creates space in your body, inviting the release of trapped energy. You may find that as you practice this technique, emotional sensations begin to surface, providing an opportunity to process and let go.

Body awareness exercises can also play a pivotal role in unlocking trauma. By tuning into specific areas of the body where tension is held, we can initiate a dialogue with ourselves that encourages release. One exercise involves finding a quiet space to sit or lie down comfortably. Focus on a part of your body that feels tight or uncomfortable—perhaps your shoulders or lower back. As you breathe into that area, visualize warmth and light flowing in, loosening any grip of tension. You might even want to gently massage the area or apply pressure with your hands, allowing the sensations to guide you. As you hold space for this discomfort, notice any emotions or memories that arise. This practice fosters a deep sense of connection to your body and encourages the release of emotional weight.

Grounding exercises are essential for returning to a place of safety and stability after experiencing the often turbulent feelings that arise during somatic practices. One effective grounding technique is to find a comfortable position while seated or standing and focus on your feet. Feel the ground beneath you, connecting with its solidity and support. Imagine roots extending from your feet deep into the earth, anchoring you firmly. As you do this, visualize any excess energy or tension flowing down through those roots, leaving your body and dissipating into the ground. This practice not only helps release stored trauma but also reinforces a sense of stability and security, allowing you to navigate the healing journey with confidence.

Incorporating movement practices, like yoga or tai chi, can also provide a gentle way to release trauma stored in the body. These disciplines emphasize fluidity and mindfulness, encouraging you to connect with your body's rhythms while moving through space. As you engage in these practices, pay attention to how certain postures resonate with your emotional state. Perhaps a forward fold evokes feelings of surrender, while a strong warrior pose instills a sense of empowerment. By honoring the physical sensations that arise during these movements, you can begin to process and release what no longer serves you.

Ultimately, the process of releasing stored trauma through somatic therapy is a dance between awareness, movement, and breath. It invites you to embrace your body as a vital partner in your healing journey, offering you a pathway to reclaim your energy and restore your sense of peace. As you engage in these practices, remember that it's a journey—one that requires patience and self-compassion. Each step you take toward understanding and releasing trauma is a testament to your resilience and your commitment to a brighter, more integrated self. You're not just navigating the terrain of trauma; you're actively participating in your own healing, and that is a powerful thing.

POLYVAGAL THEORY
The Key to Understanding Stress Responses

Let's dive into an incredibly fascinating concept that can truly illuminate our understanding of how our bodies respond to stress and trauma: Polyvagal Theory. At its core, this theory, developed by Dr. Stephen Porges, focuses on the vagus nerve, which is a key player in our nervous system. Imagine the vagus nerve as a long, winding highway that runs from the brain down through the neck and into the chest and abdomen, connecting various organs along the way. It's like a master switchboard, communicating between the brain and the body, helping to regulate vital functions such as heart rate, digestion, and our stress responses.

When we experience stress or trauma, our bodies react in a very instinctive way. We may go into fight-or-flight mode, feeling a rush of adrenaline as our bodies prepare to either confront danger or escape from it. This response is a protective mechanism, ensuring that we can respond quickly to threats. However, when these stressors become overwhelming or chronic, our nervous system can get stuck in this heightened state of alert, making it difficult to return to a place of calm. This is where Polyvagal Theory comes into play, as it helps us understand the different branches of the vagus nerve and how they impact our ability to regulate stress.

The theory highlights three main states of our nervous system: the social engagement state, the sympathetic state, and the shutdown state. In the social engagement state, we feel safe and connected, which allows us to interact with others, express emotions, and foster relationships. In contrast, the sympathetic state, which corresponds to that fight-or-flight response, is when we feel threatened, leading to increased heart rate and heightened arousal. Finally, the shutdown state is a response to overwhelming stress, where the body can feel frozen or numb. Understanding these states can empower you to recognize where you are in any given moment and how to navigate your way back to safety.

Now, how does this all tie into trauma recovery? The vagus nerve plays a crucial role in helping us regulate our stress responses and find that sense of safety again. Somatic therapy taps into this by engaging the vagus nerve in a gentle and supportive way. Techniques such as deep breathing, grounding exercises, and mindful movement can stimulate the vagus nerve, signaling to your body that it's safe to relax and let go of the fight-or-flight response. These practices invite you to reconnect with your body, fostering a sense of safety and presence that is often lost in the wake of trauma.

As you engage in somatic practices, you might notice changes in your body—perhaps a deepening of your breath, a gradual softening of tense muscles, or a sense of lightness as your mind begins to quiet. These shifts are powerful signals that your body is beginning to downregulate its stress response, allowing you to step out of that heightened state of alertness and into a more grounded, connected space. By learning to listen to your body and respond to its needs, you empower yourself to reclaim the peace and calm that is inherently yours.

It's important to remember that healing is not a linear journey. There will be ups and downs, moments when you feel like you're moving forward and others when it may seem like you've taken a step back. That's completely natural. What's essential is that you approach this process with patience and self-compassion. Engaging the vagus nerve through somatic therapy offers you a pathway to nurture your body's natural ability to heal, supporting you in cultivating resilience and strength as you navigate your trauma recovery journey. You are not just a passive observer in this process; you are an active participant, learning to tune into your body's wisdom and respond with care. And as you do, you'll find that you can emerge from the shadows of trauma with a renewed sense of self and a deeper connection to the world around you.

Chapter 2

Reclaiming Your Body
First Steps in Somatic Awareness

Somatic awareness is a profound practice that invites us to reconnect with our bodies, acknowledging the vital role they play in our emotional and psychological well-being. At its core, somatic awareness involves tuning into the sensations that arise within our physical selves, offering us a window into the way emotions, stress, and trauma manifest and are stored in our bodies. It's about becoming curious about the subtle vibrations, tightness, or even moments of lightness that we experience throughout our day. This process encourages us to cultivate a deeper understanding of how our physical state reflects our mental and emotional landscapes.

In the context of trauma recovery, somatic awareness serves as a crucial tool for healing. Traumatic experiences can leave imprints in the body, often resulting in tension, discomfort, or numbness in certain areas. By developing somatic awareness, we begin to recognize these physical sensations not as nuisances to be ignored but as important signals that our bodies are communicating. For instance, you might notice a tightness in your chest when you're feeling anxious or a heaviness in your limbs when you recall a distressing memory. These sensations are not just random occurrences; they are reflections of our emotional states, deeply rooted in our experiences. Learning to listen to these signals allows us to address our trauma more holistically, bridging the gap between mind and body.

As you embark on this journey of developing somatic awareness, you may find it helpful to pause and take stock of your body at various moments throughout the day. What sensations arise when you're feeling stressed? Where do you hold tension? Are there certain areas that feel more activated or numb than others? This practice of checking in with yourself is not just an exercise in mindfulness; it's an invitation to engage with your body's wisdom. By becoming aware of where you carry tension, you can begin to trace these sensations back to the emotions and experiences that may have contributed to their existence. This practice fosters a deeper understanding of how stress and trauma are not merely psychological phenomena but physical experiences that demand our attention and care.

Recognizing emotional triggers is another powerful aspect of developing somatic awareness. Often, we react to triggers without fully understanding why they provoke such strong responses within us. Through somatic awareness, you can learn to identify these triggers by observing your physical reactions. Perhaps a particular scent evokes a memory, or a certain sound causes your heart to race. By becoming attuned to these bodily responses, you can start to unpack the layers of emotion associated with them. This insight is not just enlightening; it empowers you to respond to your triggers in healthier, more constructive ways rather than being swept away by an automatic reaction.

The benefits of cultivating somatic awareness extend beyond simply recognizing tension and triggers. This practice lays the groundwork for healing by fostering self-compassion and acceptance. As you become more attuned to your body's signals, you may find it easier to approach yourself with kindness, understanding that it's natural to hold onto tension or react strongly to certain situations. This compassionate awareness creates a safe space for you to explore your feelings without judgment, allowing for deeper emotional processing and release.

Additionally, developing somatic awareness can enhance your ability to engage in self-soothing practices. When you can identify areas of tension or discomfort, you can respond with intentional actions— be it through breathwork, gentle movement, or relaxation techniques that help release that stored stress. This self-regulation fosters a sense of agency and empowerment, allowing you to take charge of your healing journey.

By embracing somatic awareness, you are not just recognizing the physical manifestations of your trauma; you are actively participating in your recovery. It invites you to see your body as a partner in healing rather than an adversary. As you cultivate this awareness, you will find that your body can guide you toward greater understanding, resilience, and ultimately, a more integrated sense of self. This journey is not about erasing the past; it's about honoring your experiences and reclaiming your body's innate capacity for healing.

How to Listen to Your Body's Signals

Becoming attuned to the signals your body is sending is a vital step in the journey toward healing from trauma. Our bodies are often like a finely tuned instrument, capable of conveying messages that we may not consciously recognize. Physical sensations, such as tightness, heat, or numbness, can serve as profound indicators of stored trauma. These sensations aren't merely discomforts; they are echoes of experiences that need acknowledgment and care. By learning to interpret these signals with curiosity instead of fear, you can embark on a transformative path toward deeper self-awareness and healing.

Imagine for a moment that you're sitting quietly, allowing yourself to tune into your body. As you close your eyes, take a deep breath, and notice where your attention is drawn. Do you feel tightness in your shoulders or a fluttering in your stomach? Perhaps there's a sense of heat radiating from your chest or numbness in your hands. Each of these sensations tells a story, and the key is to approach them with a sense of curiosity, as if you're gently asking your body what it needs to express. This kind of exploration encourages a dialogue between your mind and body, fostering an understanding of how they work in tandem.

When you encounter sensations like tightness, it's helpful to consider what might be at the root of it. Tightness in the chest can signal anxiety or a feeling of being overwhelmed, while tightness in the jaw might indicate suppressed emotions or tension. Instead of brushing these feelings aside or labeling them as negative, invite them in. Ask yourself, "What am I feeling right now?" or "What does this tightness remind me of?" It can be revealing to reflect on whether the sensations arise from current stressors or resonate with past experiences. Acknowledging these connections can be the first step in unraveling the layers of stored trauma.

Heat can be another powerful indicator. It might feel like warmth spreading across your face or a flush in your cheeks, often associated with feelings of anger or frustration. Instead of reacting to this sensation with avoidance, lean into it. Notice how it feels—where it is concentrated, how it ebbs and flows. Does it make you feel more alive, or does it trigger a sense of anxiety? By consciously observing these feelings, you start to build a relationship with your body, allowing it to communicate more freely.

Numbness, on the other hand, can be particularly challenging. It may feel like a disconnect, where parts of your body seem unresponsive or distant. This sensation can be a protective mechanism, a way your body shields you from overwhelming feelings. Rather than pushing this numbness away, practice sitting with it for a few moments. Breathe into the areas where you feel numb and gently ask your body what it needs. This isn't about forcing a response but rather about creating a space for awareness and understanding. Over time, this practice can help re-establish a connection with those parts of yourself that may feel shut off.

To make this process a part of your daily routine, consider setting aside moments throughout your day to check in with yourself. It could be as simple as pausing during your morning coffee or taking a minute between tasks to breathe and notice your body. Ask yourself what sensations are present—are there areas of tension or relaxation? Over time, this practice will train your mind to recognize the signals your body sends, making it easier to respond to them with compassion.

Mindfulness exercises can also enhance your attunement to bodily sensations. Try simple practices like body scans, where you focus your attention sequentially on each part of your body, noting any sensations without judgment. You might find it helpful to do this at the end of the day, reflecting on your experiences and how your body responded to them. Journaling can also be a valuable tool in this process. Write down your observations, noting the sensations you felt and any emotional responses that arose. This reflective practice not only deepens your understanding but also tracks your journey toward greater self-awareness.

As you engage with your body's signals, remember to be patient and gentle with yourself. Healing is not a linear path, and it's perfectly normal to experience moments of resistance or discomfort. Each sensation you encounter is an opportunity for exploration, a chance to better understand the relationship between your mind and body. By embracing this journey with curiosity, you're not just listening to your body; you're fostering a deeper, more compassionate connection with yourself. And as you learn to trust this connection, you'll find that the road to healing becomes a little less daunting and a lot more empowering.

Identifying Areas of Tension and Stress

Performing a body scan is a gentle yet powerful way to tune into your body's wisdom and become aware of areas that may be holding tension, discomfort, or stress. This practice invites you to bring your attention inward, creating a space where you can simply observe what's happening within you without judgment. As you embark on this journey, I encourage you to find a quiet, comfortable spot where you can relax, free from distractions. You might choose to lie down or sit in a supportive chair, allowing your body to feel supported by the ground or the surface beneath you. When you're ready, take a deep breath in through your nose, filling your lungs completely, and then exhale slowly through your mouth, releasing any initial tension.

Let's begin at the very top—your head. Bring your awareness to your scalp and notice any sensations there. Is it tight? Relaxed? Just observe without needing to change anything. Allow your focus to gently drift to your forehead, noticing if there's any tension or furrowing of the brow. As you breathe deeply, let your exhale soften any tightness you may feel. Move down to your eyes and cheeks, allowing them to relax. Feel the weight of your eyelids. Are they heavy or light? Perhaps you notice the tiny muscles around your eyes that may hold stress. Let go of any clenching as you breathe out.

Now, guide your awareness to your jaw. This area often holds a significant amount of tension. You might find that your teeth are clenched or your jaw is tight. If so, try gently parting your lips slightly, letting your jaw hang loose, and notice how that feels. As you take another breath in and out, imagine sending your breath to that area, softening it further with each exhale. As you continue down your neck, pay attention to any stiffness or discomfort. Allow your shoulders to drop away from your ears, releasing the weight they might be carrying.

Take a moment here to consciously relax each muscle in your neck and shoulders, inviting a sense of ease into these areas.

Next, move your focus to your chest and upper back. Notice the rise and fall of your breath. Are there any tightness or sensations present? Perhaps a feeling of constriction or openness? Allow your breath to flow freely, visualizing it expanding through your chest, creating space where you might feel any heaviness. As you breathe, gently release any areas of tension, inviting softness and comfort into this part of your body.

Shift your attention to your abdomen. The belly is often a place where we store emotions, and it can be helpful to observe how it feels. Is it tense or relaxed? Notice how your breath moves in and out of your belly. As you breathe in, feel it expand; as you exhale, allow it to contract gently. If you notice any discomfort, simply acknowledge it, breathing into that area and giving yourself permission to let go.

Continue your journey down to your hips and lower back. These areas are often associated with carrying stress or burdens. Do you feel tightness or discomfort? Allow yourself to visualize releasing any heaviness as you breathe out. Picture the tension melting away, leaving space for relaxation. As you move further down, bring your awareness to your thighs and knees. Pay attention to any sensations here. You might feel the weight of your legs or a tightness in your muscles. Invite that tension to dissolve with each breath, letting go of any lingering stress.

Next, direct your focus to your calves and ankles. Notice how they feel in relation to the surface beneath you. Are they heavy or light? Is there a sense of relaxation, or do you feel tightness? Allow your breath to wash over these areas, releasing tension with each exhale. Finally, bring your awareness to your feet. Feel the connection between your feet and the ground, anchoring you. Observe any sensations, perhaps tingling or heaviness. As you breathe into your feet, imagine sending down roots, grounding yourself more deeply into the earth.

As you complete this body scan, take a moment to reflect on the journey you just took through your body. What did you notice? Did any emotions arise as you scanned different areas? This practice is not just about identifying tension; it's also about cultivating mindfulness and compassion toward yourself. Acknowledge whatever you experienced without judgment. Perhaps you found areas of tightness that need your attention, or maybe you felt moments of relief and relaxation. Whatever the case, know that this practice can be a valuable tool in your healing journey, allowing you to tune in, listen, and respond to your body's needs with kindness and care.

Mindful Breathing: Calming the Nervous System

Mindful breathing is a simple yet transformative practice that serves as a powerful tool for calming the nervous system and anchoring our awareness in the present moment. In the midst of life's chaos and the weight of past traumas, many of us find ourselves caught in a cycle of anxiety, worry, or racing thoughts. This is where the magic of mindful breathing comes into play. By focusing on our breath, we create a bridge to the present, allowing ourselves to step away from the noise of the mind and reconnect with our bodies. It's a gentle reminder that, no matter how turbulent our thoughts may be, we always have the breath as a source of grounding and comfort.

To begin this journey, let's explore a few simple breathing techniques that you can weave into your daily routine. One effective method is diaphragmatic breathing, often called belly breathing. To practice this, find a comfortable position, either sitting or lying down. Place one hand on your chest and the other on your belly. Inhale deeply through your nose, allowing your belly to expand while keeping your chest relatively still. This full, deep breath engages your diaphragm and fills your lungs, creating a sense of fullness and calm. As you exhale slowly through your mouth, feel your belly deflate. With each breath, you'll notice a natural rhythm emerging, and as you focus on this cycle, the tension in your body will begin to melt away.

Another technique is box breathing, which is wonderfully effective for managing stress and promoting relaxation. To practice this, imagine drawing a box in the air with your breath. Inhale deeply for a count of four, feeling your lungs fill with air. Hold your breath for another count of four, then exhale slowly for four counts, releasing any stress with each breath out. Finally, pause at the bottom of the exhale for a count of four before inhaling again. This rhythmic pattern not only calms the nervous system but also helps sharpen your focus, making it a great tool during particularly overwhelming moments.

As you engage in these mindful breathing exercises, you may notice something remarkable: your body begins to activate its parasympathetic nervous system. This is often referred to as the "rest and digest" system, and it plays a crucial role in promoting relaxation and healing. When we breathe mindfully, we send signals to our body that it is safe to relax. The heart rate slows, blood pressure decreases, and the mind begins to clear. This physiological shift is essential for trauma recovery, as it allows us to create a sense of safety and ease that may have been disrupted by past experiences.

Mindful breathing does more than just help us feel better in the moment; it lays the foundation for a deeper connection with ourselves. By taking time to breathe intentionally, we cultivate a practice of self-awareness and self-compassion. Each breath becomes an invitation to be present with our feelings, to acknowledge what we are experiencing without judgment. This gentle approach fosters an environment where healing can occur, helping us to release what no longer serves us and to nurture a greater sense of peace within.

Incorporating mindful breathing into your life can be as simple as taking a few moments throughout your day to check in with your breath. Whether you're facing a challenging situation, feeling overwhelmed, or simply wanting to reconnect with yourself, these techniques can be your lifeline. So, let's embrace the power of our breath and allow it to guide us toward a more peaceful, centered existence.

Chapter 3

Grounding Techniques – How to Feel Safe in Your Body Again

eing "grounded" is a term that often evokes a feeling of stability, calm, and presence within the body. It's that reassuring sense of being firmly connected to the earth beneath us, as if we're drawing strength from the ground and feeling secure in our own skin. When we are grounded, we're not just physically aware; we're also emotionally centered, able to navigate our surroundings with a clear mind and an open heart. It's that beautiful state where our thoughts, feelings, and physical sensations harmonize, allowing us to experience life fully and authentically.

For those who have experienced trauma, the journey to feeling grounded can be particularly challenging. Trauma often creates a profound disconnection between the mind and body. In the aftermath of a traumatic event, many people find themselves feeling detached, numb, or dissociated, as if they're observing their life from a distance rather than truly participating in it. This disconnection can manifest in various ways—maybe it's a sense of floating through daily tasks, an inability to recognize physical sensations, or an overwhelming feeling of being lost and out of control. The body, which is supposed to be a source of strength and comfort, can instead feel like a foreign entity, disconnected from our sense of self.

This is where grounding techniques come into play, serving as a lifeline to restore that vital connection. Grounding practices help individuals reconnect with their bodies and their immediate environment, allowing them to reclaim a sense of safety and presence. These techniques can be as simple as taking a moment to focus on the sensation of your feet on the ground, feeling the texture of the earth beneath you, or practicing mindful breathing to bring attention back to your body. Each grounding exercise is a gentle reminder that you are here, in this moment, and that you have the power to influence how you feel.

As you engage in grounding practices, you might notice a shift within yourself. The chaos of anxious thoughts may begin to settle, and that once-overwhelming sense of disconnection can fade. You might start to feel a warmth spread through your body, a lightness in your chest, or even a sense of relief washing over you. This is the beauty of grounding—it invites you to experience your body as a safe haven rather than a battleground. By nurturing this connection, you not only enhance your emotional resilience but also cultivate a deeper understanding of your physical self, laying the groundwork for healing and recovery.

In essence, grounding is not just about feeling stable; it's about reclaiming your life from the grip of trauma. It's an invitation to step back into your body and rediscover the inherent strength and wisdom it holds. Through grounding techniques, you can slowly but surely mend the fractures left by trauma, restoring a sense of safety that allows you to face each day with renewed courage and hope.

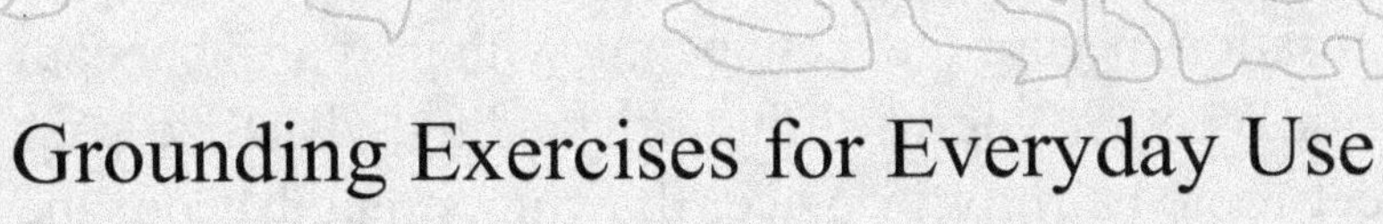

Grounding Exercises for Everyday Use

Grounding exercises are a fantastic way to help you stay present and connected to your body, especially during moments of stress, anxiety, or emotional overwhelm. One of the simplest and most effective techniques you can use is the "5-4-3-2-1" method. This exercise encourages you to engage your senses, pulling your attention away from distressing thoughts and into the here and now. To practice this, start by looking around and naming five things you can see. Maybe it's the vibrant color of a nearby plant, the way light dances on a surface, or even the texture of your clothing. Next, focus on four things you can touch—perhaps the coolness of the chair you're sitting on, the softness of a blanket, or the feel of your hands resting in your lap. Then, shift to three things you can hear. This might be the distant sound of traffic, birds chirping outside, or the gentle hum of a fan. Follow that by identifying two things you can smell; if you can't pick up a scent right away, it's perfectly okay to think of a favorite fragrance. Finally, bring your awareness to one thing you can taste, which could be the lingering flavor of your last meal or a sip of water. By consciously engaging your senses, you redirect your focus and foster a sense of calm in the present moment.

Another grounding technique is simply feeling your feet on the ground. Take a moment to pause and notice the sensation of your feet connecting with the earth beneath you. Whether you're sitting or standing, visualize your feet rooted firmly in place, drawing strength from the ground. Pay attention to how the weight of your body is distributed and the way your feet support you. You might even imagine your feet as tree roots, extending deep into the earth, anchoring you securely. This visualization can be particularly soothing, helping to reduce feelings of anxiety by reminding you of your physical presence and stability.

In addition to these methods, you can practice deep breathing to enhance your grounding experience. Close your eyes if you feel comfortable, and take a slow, deep breath in through your nose, allowing your belly to expand fully. Hold that breath for a moment, and then gently exhale through your mouth, feeling your body relax with each out-breath. As you breathe, you can mentally connect your breath to your feet, envisioning your inhalation drawing in calm and grounding energy, while your exhalation releases tension and anxiety. This rhythmic connection between breath and body not only calms the nervous system but also anchors you in the present.

When stress or overwhelming emotions arise, these grounding exercises can be your lifeline. They remind you that even in turbulent moments, you have the power to reconnect with yourself and the environment around you. By incorporating these techniques into your daily life, whether during a hectic day at work or a quiet moment at home, you cultivate a sense of awareness and resilience that supports your overall well-being. Embrace these exercises as tools you can use anytime you need to pause, reflect, and return to a place of calm.

Using Your Environment to Anchor Yourself

Creating a sense of grounding and safety in your surroundings can be a powerful tool for managing overwhelming emotions and interrupting feelings of dissociation. When you find yourself feeling anxious or disconnected, turning your attention to the world around you can help anchor you back to the present moment. Start by choosing a comfortable spot, whether you're inside or outside. Look around and pick a physical object to focus on. It could be a chair, a plant, or even a piece of art. Allow yourself to take a moment to really observe it—notice its colors, shapes, and textures. As you do this, breathe deeply and let your breath flow in sync with your observations. This simple act of focusing on an object can draw your attention away from distressing thoughts and into the here and now.

Another effective way to ground yourself is by engaging with the textures in your environment. Run your fingers over a soft blanket, feel the coolness of a metal surface, or touch the warmth of a wooden table. Notice how these sensations feel against your skin. Pay attention to the details—the way the fabric feels, the temperature of the material, and any subtle changes you notice as you touch it. By immersing yourself in these sensory experiences, you create a tangible connection to your surroundings, which can provide a soothing sense of safety and stability.

Sound is another powerful anchor. Take a moment to listen closely to the sounds around you. It could be the gentle rustling of leaves outside, the rhythmic ticking of a clock, or even the distant hum of traffic. Close your eyes if it helps, and let yourself focus entirely on the soundscape. Try to identify as many distinct sounds as you can. Each sound can serve as a reminder that you are present and safe in your environment, helping to diminish feelings of anxiety or panic.

Sight, too, can be a grounding tool. Take a deep breath and focus on the colors in your environment. Maybe it's the vibrant green of a houseplant, the soft beige of your walls, or the intricate patterns of a rug. Allow yourself to explore the details—the way light interacts with these colors, the shadows they create, and how they change as the day goes on. This exercise encourages you to slow down and appreciate the beauty around you, reminding you that there is much to take in, even amidst distress.

Anchoring to your environment can serve as a helpful interruption when emotions feel overwhelming. If you notice yourself becoming dissociated or lost in a wave of anxiety, redirecting your focus to your surroundings can bring you back to the present. It's like giving your mind a gentle nudge, saying, "Here I am. I'm safe, and I can find solace in this moment." The practice of anchoring is not just about the immediate relief it offers; it's also about fostering a deeper relationship with your environment. By learning to recognize and appreciate the details of your surroundings, you create a sense of familiarity and safety that can help stabilize you during challenging times.

Embracing these techniques can transform how you navigate your day-to-day life. With time and practice, grounding techniques can become second nature, providing you with tools to tap into whenever you need them. You are not just a passive observer in your environment; you are an active participant, capable of creating a sanctuary of safety and comfort wherever you are. As you explore these practices, you'll likely find that they not only help you in moments of stress but also enrich your overall experience of being present in the world.

How Touch, Sound, and Sight Can Help You Stay Present

Engaging the senses can be a powerful tool for grounding, helping you stay anchored in the present moment. When you immerse yourself in the sights, sounds, and textures around you, it creates a bridge to the here and now, pulling you away from anxious thoughts or overwhelming emotions. Imagine standing in your living room, surrounded by familiar objects. Take a moment to really notice what's there. Feel the texture of the fabric on your couch or the coolness of a mug in your hand. These small details remind you of your physical space and help reestablish your connection to your body.

To tap into the sense of touch, try an exercise where you explore different textures. Find a few items around you—maybe a soft blanket, a smooth stone, or a piece of rough bark. As you run your fingers over each item, pay close attention to how it feels against your skin. Is it warm or cold? Soft or hard? Let your mind focus on these sensations, allowing them to draw you away from stressful thoughts and into the tactile experience. You might be surprised at how grounding this simple act can be, creating a moment of calm amidst chaos.

Sound is another incredible way to anchor yourself in the present. Close your eyes and take a deep breath, then begin to listen. What sounds do you notice? The chirping of birds outside, the gentle hum of the refrigerator, or perhaps the distant sounds of traffic? As you identify each sound, allow yourself to focus entirely on it, letting go of distractions. You could even create a "sound map" in your mind, visualizing where each sound is coming from. This practice can help calm the nervous system, easing tension as you become fully immersed in your auditory environment.

Visual elements can also serve as a soothing balm for the mind. Look around and pick a few objects to focus on, whether it's a vibrant piece of art on the wall or the play of sunlight filtering through leaves outside. Notice the colors, shapes, and patterns. Allow your gaze to linger on these elements, taking in their beauty and detail. This act of mindful observation can shift your mental state, interrupting cycles of anxiety by directing your attention to the external world rather than internal worries.

You might also try a simple exercise where you consciously pick three colors around you and describe them in your mind. What shades are they? How do they make you feel? By intentionally focusing on the visual aspects of your environment, you're not only engaging your senses but also nurturing a sense of safety and stability in the present moment.

By cultivating sensory awareness through these exercises, you can help calm your nervous system and create a sense of balance in your body. Engaging your senses brings you back to your physical experience, reminding you that you are here, safe and secure. This practice can be particularly effective during moments of stress or when anxiety begins to creep in. As you explore your surroundings with intention, you'll likely find that it becomes easier to manage your emotions, fostering a deeper connection to yourself and the world around you.

Chapter 4

Breathwork – Reclaiming Calm Through Your Breath

The connection between breath and the nervous system is truly profound, especially in the context of trauma recovery. Breath is more than just a physiological function; it serves as a bridge between our minds and bodies. When we experience trauma, our nervous system often gets stuck in a heightened state of alertness. This is our body's way of protecting us, but it can leave us feeling anxious, overwhelmed, and disconnected from ourselves. By focusing on our breath, we can tap into a powerful tool that helps us regulate our emotions, reduce stress, and promote healing.

When we breathe deeply and consciously, we activate the parasympathetic nervous system, often referred to as the "rest and digest" system. This part of the nervous system helps to counteract the fight-or-flight response that can dominate after a traumatic experience. As we inhale and exhale slowly, we signal to our body that it is safe to relax. This simple act of breathing creates a sense of calm, allowing us to step back from the chaos of our thoughts and feelings. In essence, controlled breathing serves as a gentle reminder to our bodies that we are no longer in immediate danger.

Breathwork, which encompasses various techniques for using the breath intentionally, can be particularly effective for trauma survivors. By engaging in practices such as diaphragmatic breathing or rhythmic breath patterns, individuals can significantly decrease their levels of stress and anxiety. This is because when we breathe slowly and deeply, we lower our heart rate and reduce the production of stress hormones like cortisol. In turn, this helps to alleviate physical symptoms of stress, such as tension in the muscles, digestive issues, and a racing heart.

Moreover, breathwork can enhance emotional regulation. Many trauma survivors find themselves in a cycle of intense emotions that can feel overwhelming. Through breath-focused practices, individuals learn to create space between their thoughts and feelings, fostering a greater sense of control. When faced with distressing emotions, a few moments of intentional breathing can help ground individuals, allowing them to respond to their feelings with greater clarity and less reactivity. This becomes a vital part of the healing process, as it helps individuals reclaim their emotional stability.

Physiologically, the effects of intentional breathing on trauma survivors are remarkable. As breath patterns shift from shallow and rapid to deep and slow, the body begins to release stored tension and trauma. This shift can promote a sense of ease and safety that many survivors have longed for. Additionally, oxygenating the body through mindful breathing supports optimal brain function, which can be disrupted by trauma. Enhanced oxygen flow not only improves cognitive function but also helps to release endorphins, the body's natural feel-good chemicals. This can create a positive feedback loop, where the act of breathing promotes healing, which in turn encourages further engagement with breathwork.

By integrating breathwork into their recovery journey, trauma survivors can cultivate a more profound connection to their bodies. The breath becomes an anchor, helping to center them in the present moment and reconnect with their physical selves. This relationship with breath not only promotes healing but also empowers individuals to navigate their emotions with newfound resilience and grace. Through each inhale and exhale, they are reminded that they have the capacity to find peace and restore balance in their lives, one breath at a time.

Breathing for Calm: Simple Techniques You Can Use Anytime

When stress and anxiety hit, it can feel like everything is spiraling out of control. Your heart races, your breath becomes shallow, and it's hard to think clearly. But what if I told you there's a simple, accessible tool that can help you regain your calm, no matter where you are? Your breath. By using specific breathing techniques, you can directly influence your body's stress response, sending signals to your nervous system that it's safe to relax. Let's explore some of these practices that you can use anytime you need to ground yourself and find calm.

Diaphragmatic breathing, often called belly breathing, is a powerful way to engage the body's natural relaxation system. Most of us tend to breathe shallowly into our chest, especially when we're stressed. This kind of breathing only amplifies anxiety, as it mimics the body's response to danger. Diaphragmatic breathing invites you to slow down and take deep, full breaths, expanding your diaphragm. It's simple. Start by placing one hand on your chest and the other on your belly. As you inhale through your nose, aim to fill your belly with air, feeling it rise as your chest stays relatively still. Then, exhale slowly through your mouth, gently pressing the air out. This deep, mindful breath communicates to your brain that you're safe, helping to shift your body out of fight-or-flight mode. With practice, diaphragmatic breathing can become your go-to technique for easing anxiety in moments of stress, whether you're at home, at work, or even out in public.

Another incredibly effective method for calming the mind is box breathing, also known as square breathing. This technique is a favorite among many, including military personnel and first responders, because it's simple, portable, and works fast. Imagine a square or box, with each side representing one part of your breath. You inhale slowly for a count of four, hold the breath for a count of four, exhale for four, and hold again for four before starting over. This rhythmic pattern not only distracts your mind from anxious thoughts but also helps regulate your nervous system by promoting balance between your inhale and exhale. As you practice, you may find that your heart rate slows, your muscles begin to loosen, and a sense of calm washes over you. Box breathing can be done discreetly, making it a handy tool during meetings, stressful conversations, or even when you're lying awake in bed with racing thoughts.

If you're looking for something that feels more meditative, alternate nostril breathing offers a beautifully calming practice. Known in yoga as *Nadi Shodhana*, this technique helps bring balance to both sides of your brain and body. To begin, find a comfortable seated position. Place your right thumb on your right nostril, gently closing it off, and inhale deeply through your left nostril. At the top of your breath, close your left nostril with your right ring finger, release your thumb from the right nostril, and exhale fully. Inhale again through the right nostril, close it, and exhale through the left. Continue alternating in this way, allowing each breath to slow and deepen. This practice has a wonderfully calming effect on the mind and body, as it encourages an even flow of energy and a sense of internal harmony. It's especially helpful when you feel overwhelmed, scattered, or out of sync with yourself.

Each of these breathing techniques taps into your body's innate ability to regulate itself, offering a way to shift out of the chaos of stress and back into a state of ease. Whether you choose to engage in diaphragmatic breathing, box breathing, or alternate nostril breathing, these tools are always with you, ready to be used whenever you need them. The more you practice, the more natural they'll feel, becoming trusted companions in your journey to reduce anxiety and restore balance in your life.

Breath Awareness in Stressful Moments

When life feels overwhelming and your body tightens with stress or anxiety, one of the first things to shift is your breathing. It's so easy to miss—shallow, rapid breaths sneaking in as your mind races, leaving you feeling even more out of control. But here's the key: your breath is not just a reflection of what you're feeling, it's also a powerful tool you can use to regain a sense of calm. Developing an awareness of your breath is like having a quiet anchor in the middle of the storm. It doesn't demand anything from you. It's always there, waiting for you to notice.

When you're stressed or anxious, your body enters a state of heightened alertness, and one of the most immediate signs of this is irregular or shallow breathing. You might notice your breaths becoming quick and sharp, or perhaps you're even unconsciously holding your breath, bracing yourself against the tension in your body. These subtle changes in your breathing are your body's way of telling you that it's in survival mode, preparing you for what it perceives as a threat, even if that threat is just a pile of work or an emotionally charged situation. Becoming aware of this shift is a crucial first step. By simply noticing when your breath becomes short or uneven, you're already moving toward a place of greater control and self-regulation.

The beauty of breath awareness is that it doesn't require any special equipment or a lot of time. In those moments when stress has a grip on you, take a second to just pause. You don't need to force anything. Just notice. What does your breath feel like right now? Where do you feel it most? Is it shallow, sitting in your chest, or does it reach down into your belly? This small act of tuning in can interrupt the automatic stress response and invite your mind and body back to the present moment.

Once you've noticed how stress affects your breath, you can gently begin to guide it toward a calmer rhythm. Try shifting your focus to taking deeper, slower breaths. Inhale through your nose and let the air fill your belly, rather than just your chest. Let the breath expand your abdomen like a balloon. As you exhale, do so slowly and fully, as though you're releasing the tension that's been building inside. Imagine each breath as a wave, washing away a little more of the stress each time. The exhale, especially, is where your body begins to let go. It's where relaxation lives.

You don't have to make this a dramatic shift. Even small, conscious adjustments to your breath can have a profound impact. Sometimes, just counting to four on the inhale and to six or eight on the exhale can help extend the breath and slow everything down. The slower and deeper your breath becomes, the more your nervous system starts to shift from fight-or-flight mode back to a state of rest and recovery. This is the power of mindful breathing—it turns off the alarm bells ringing in your body and signals that it's safe to relax.

Advanced Breathwork for Deep Healing

As you continue to explore somatic therapy for trauma recovery, you may feel ready to go beyond the foundational breathing techniques and venture into more advanced breathwork practices. Techniques like Holotropic Breathwork or SOMA Breathwork offer profound tools for those seeking a deeper level of emotional release and healing. Unlike basic breathing exercises, which primarily focus on grounding and calming the nervous system, these advanced methods dive into the subconscious layers of stored trauma, allowing you to access and process emotions that might otherwise remain trapped in your body.

Holotropic Breathwork, developed by psychiatrist Dr. Stanislav Grof, is a powerful technique designed to induce altered states of consciousness through accelerated, rhythmic breathing. This practice mirrors the heightened breath rate often associated with intense emotional experiences. By intentionally engaging in this deep, rapid breathing, you can bypass the thinking mind and access repressed emotions, memories, and sensations. Many describe the experience as a journey into the psyche, where they are able to confront and release trauma that traditional therapies may not reach. The practice is typically done in a supportive group setting or under the guidance of a trained facilitator who creates a safe, contained space for emotional expression. Sessions often include evocative music and bodywork to encourage further release.

SOMA Breathwork shares some similarities but is designed with a slightly different focus. It incorporates rhythmic breathing patterns, often synchronized with music, to create a meditative, trance-like state. SOMA emphasizes a balance between hyper-oxygenation and breath retention to induce calm and clarity while also facilitating emotional release. This practice works to harmonize the brain's hemispheres, which can help trauma survivors reconnect with their bodies and reduce the feeling of fragmentation that trauma often brings. Like Holotropic Breathwork, SOMA encourages a deeper connection to the self, unlocking suppressed emotions and facilitating healing at a cellular level.

While these techniques hold immense potential for emotional release, it's essential to approach them with care, especially if you have experienced significant trauma. The intensity of these practices can sometimes bring up powerful and raw emotions that may be overwhelming if not properly prepared for. This is why working with a trained practitioner is highly recommended, particularly in the early stages of exploring these advanced breathwork methods. A skilled facilitator can guide you through the process, ensuring that you feel safe and supported throughout the experience. They can also help you integrate any insights or emotional releases that arise, so the healing becomes part of your ongoing journey rather than something that feels isolating or destabilizing.

If you're practicing on your own, make sure to ease into these techniques gradually, especially if you're new to more intense breathwork. Begin by creating a quiet, safe space where you won't be disturbed. Start with shorter sessions, paying attention to how your body responds, and be sure to take breaks if emotions become too intense. Remember, it's not about forcing the process—your body will release emotions at its own pace. Practicing regularly, even for short periods, can build resilience and comfort with the technique, allowing you to access deeper layers of healing as you feel ready.

Holotropic and SOMA Breathwork have the potential to unlock emotional layers that might seem unreachable through talk therapy or basic relaxation exercises. These practices offer a pathway to reclaiming the body and processing trauma in a way that feels deeply personal and transformative. Just remember to approach this journey with the same compassion and patience you've developed through your other somatic practices. Breathwork, like healing itself, is not a race—it's a process that unfolds in its own time, offering you exactly what you need in each moment.

Chapter 5

Gentle Movement – Releasing Trauma Through the Body

Movement plays a crucial role in trauma recovery because our bodies often hold onto the experiences of trauma long after the mind has processed them. When we face traumatic events, our natural response can be to freeze, either physically or emotionally. This freezing is the body's way of protecting us, bracing for impact, or preparing for survival. Over time, however, these protective responses can leave behind layers of tension, stiffness, and restricted movement that manifest in ways we may not fully understand.

Trauma can create a sense of being "stuck" in the body. You might notice that your muscles feel tight or that your posture has changed. Perhaps certain areas of your body feel numb, heavy, or perpetually tense. These sensations are often the result of trauma being stored physically, which can create a feeling of being trapped or frozen in time. When this happens, our body may continue to react to situations as if the trauma is still occurring, even though the immediate danger has passed. This state of hypervigilance can lead to chronic pain, headaches, digestive issues, or just an overall sense of unease.

Gentle movement offers a pathway to begin releasing this stored tension and stress. By consciously engaging with your body, you allow it to unfreeze and re-enter a state of flow. Simple movements, such as stretching, walking, or mindful breathing, can slowly coax the body back into feeling safe and relaxed. Movement helps reconnect the mind with the body, reminding both that the trauma is over, and it's okay to let go. It's not about forcing or pushing the body through intense exercise; rather, it's about listening to what feels comfortable, slowly expanding your range of motion, and inviting your body to release what it's been holding.

In trauma recovery, movement also serves as a way to reestablish a sense of control. Trauma often leaves us feeling powerless, and by taking small, deliberate actions—whether that's rolling your shoulders or swaying from side to side—you remind yourself that you are in control of your body now. This act of reclaiming your body, through something as simple as stretching or deep breathing, can have profound psychological and emotional effects. Over time, movement becomes more than just a physical release; it becomes a way of building trust with your body, helping you feel more grounded and present.

Gentle Stretching to Release Tension

When it comes to releasing the physical tension stored in our bodies from trauma, gentle stretching can be a powerful tool. Trauma often settles in areas like the neck, shoulders, and lower back, creating tightness and discomfort that can impact both our physical and emotional well-being. By bringing movement and breath to these areas, you can begin to unlock that tension, inviting relaxation and a sense of release.

Let's start with a simple neck stretch. Begin by finding a comfortable seat, whether in a chair or on the floor, making sure your spine is tall and your shoulders are relaxed. Gently let your right ear drop towards your right shoulder, keeping your shoulders soft and away from your ears. You may feel a stretch along the left side of your neck—let it be gentle, no forcing here. If it feels right, extend your left arm down by your side or gently place your right hand on the side of your head for a deeper stretch. Hold this position for a few slow breaths, allowing your exhales to encourage the release of tension. When you're ready, slowly return to center, and repeat on the other side. This stretch helps ease the tightness that tends to accumulate in the neck and upper shoulders, areas often affected by stress and emotional strain.

For your shoulders, try a shoulder roll exercise. Sit or stand comfortably with your arms relaxed at your sides. As you inhale, slowly lift your shoulders towards your ears. On the exhale, roll them back and down, creating a circular motion with your shoulders. This rolling action helps to release the chronic tension that often builds up in this area, while also improving circulation and opening up the chest. You can reverse the motion by rolling your shoulders forward if that feels good for you. Take a few moments to notice how this simple movement feels, and remember to sync it with your breath—inhale as you lift, exhale as you release.

Next, let's focus on the lower back, an area where many of us store physical stress. For this, a seated forward fold can offer relief. Sit on the floor with your legs extended straight out in front of you. Inhale and lengthen your spine, reaching your arms up overhead. As you exhale, hinge forward from your hips, allowing your hands to rest wherever they naturally fall—on your thighs, shins, or feet. Keep your spine long and avoid rounding your back, focusing more on the sensation of stretching the lower back and hamstrings rather than how far you can fold. Breathe deeply here, feeling the gentle stretch in your lower back, and with each exhale, see if you can soften a little more. This movement helps to release tension in the lower spine and hips, areas that can feel tight or even locked when we've experienced trauma.

For deeper relaxation and a focus on the entire body, try a lying down twist. Lie on your back with your knees bent and feet flat on the floor. Extend your arms out to your sides in a T-shape, palms facing up. On an exhale, let both knees slowly drop to the right, keeping your shoulders pressed gently into the floor. If it feels good, you can turn your head to the left to enhance the twist. Hold here, breathing deeply into your belly, and feel the stretch in your lower back, hips, and spine. After a few breaths, gently bring your knees back to center and repeat on the other side. Twisting is a wonderful way to decompress the spine and release tension that may be hiding deep in the muscles around the lower back and hips.

Another stretch that can provide significant relief is the shoulder opener. For this, stand tall with your feet hip-width apart and clasp your hands behind your back. Straighten your arms and, on an inhale, gently lift your chest as you squeeze your shoulder blades together. Imagine your heart opening as your shoulders roll back and down, creating space across your chest. Hold here for a few breaths, allowing your shoulders to soften and expand. If it feels safe, you can deepen the stretch by folding forward at your hips, letting your arms reach overhead and stretching through the shoulders. This movement helps counteract the effects of hunching forward—something many of us do when we feel stressed, anxious, or protective of our emotional space.

Finally, let's close with a stretch that targets the hips, which are known to be a storage center for emotional tension. Begin by coming into a low lunge position with your right foot forward and left knee resting on the floor behind you. Make sure your front knee is stacked over your ankle, and place your hands on your front thigh for support. Take a deep breath in, and as you exhale, gently press your hips forward, feeling a stretch along the front of your left hip and thigh. This is where many of us carry the weight of stress and trauma, and opening up this space can provide profound relief. Stay here for several breaths, allowing your hips to slowly release, and then switch to the other side when you're ready.

These stretches not only help to release physical tension but also create space for emotional healing. By moving with intention and focusing on your breath, you're giving your body the gentle support it needs to let go of what it's holding onto. As you practice, allow yourself to feel the release, knowing that each stretch is a step toward reclaiming comfort in your body.

Introduction to Somatic Yoga

Somatic yoga is a gentle, trauma-informed approach to movement that offers a way to reconnect with your body in a safe and supportive environment. Unlike traditional yoga, where the focus can sometimes be on achieving certain poses or physical goals, somatic yoga invites you to slow down and explore your body's sensations with curiosity and compassion. It's a practice rooted in mindfulness, designed to help you develop a deeper awareness of your body, breath, and emotions, which is especially important for those recovering from trauma.

Trauma often leaves its imprint in the body, causing tension, discomfort, or even a sense of disconnection. Somatic yoga seeks to address this by guiding you through slow, mindful movements that are less about reaching a final pose and more about noticing how your body feels as you move. Each movement becomes an opportunity to listen to your body's signals, to observe where you might be holding tension, and to release it gradually. In this way, somatic yoga is less performance-based and more experiential. There is no right or wrong way to move—just your way, in that moment.

A typical somatic yoga practice might begin with a few moments of stillness, allowing you to settle into your space and become aware of your body. You might start by noticing the rhythm of your breath or the way your body connects with the ground beneath you. As you move through the practice, the emphasis is on slow, deliberate motions that allow you to stay present with the sensations in your body. Movements are often small and subtle, but incredibly profound in their ability to release tension and promote a sense of inner calm.

For example, a beginner-level pose that you might try is the "Somatic Cat-Cow," a gentle variation of the traditional Cat-Cow stretch. As you move between arching your back and rounding it, the focus in somatic yoga is not on how far you can go, but on how the movement feels in your spine. You might close your eyes to enhance your internal focus, moving slowly and pausing to notice any areas of tightness or ease. The key is to listen to your body and adjust the movement to match what feels right for you in the moment.

Another beginner sequence could involve a "Somatic Forward Fold." Instead of striving to reach your toes, you'll bend forward only as far as feels comfortable, paying attention to the stretch in your hamstrings and lower back. The emphasis here is on softening into the pose, using your breath to release tension rather than forcing your body to go deeper. As you inhale, you might gently rise back up halfway, lengthening your spine, and as you exhale, fold back down with a sense of ease and surrender.

Safety and self-compassion are central to somatic yoga. There is no push to achieve; instead, you are encouraged to honor your body's boundaries and move in a way that feels nourishing. If you feel discomfort or pain, it's a signal to modify the movement or take a break. Somatic yoga is about giving yourself permission to rest when needed and trusting that your body knows what it needs in each moment. This practice teaches you to befriend your body, to offer it kindness, and to rebuild a sense of safety within yourself.

As you explore somatic yoga, you may notice subtle shifts in how you experience your body. Movements may start to feel more fluid, and over time, you might find yourself becoming more attuned to your body's cues both on and off the mat. In this practice, there is no rush—only a gentle invitation to move with awareness and compassion, one breath at a time.

Mindful Walking: Healing Step by Step

Mindful walking is a beautiful and accessible way to integrate gentle movement with somatic awareness. It's not about the destination but about slowing down and reconnecting with your body, step by step. Imagine walking not just as a means of getting somewhere, but as a form of healing—a moment where your body, mind, and breath come together in harmony. As you begin this practice, the goal is to invite a sense of presence into every movement, paying attention to the sensations that arise in your body as each foot meets the ground.

To start, find a quiet place where you can walk without distractions. This could be a park, your backyard, or even a hallway in your home. Begin by standing still for a moment, letting your feet root into the earth. Feel the solidity beneath you, how the ground supports you. Take a few deep breaths, allowing your body to settle and your mind to slow down. Notice how your weight shifts from one foot to the other, how your legs support you effortlessly. This grounding moment is a reminder that you are held by the earth, that you can trust it to carry your weight, no matter how heavy or light you feel.

As you start to walk, slow your pace. This isn't a hurried or mechanical movement, but rather a gentle, intentional step forward. With each step, bring your attention to your feet. Feel the sensation of your heel touching the ground, then the ball of your foot, and finally your toes. Notice the subtle shifts in weight and balance as you transfer from one foot to the other. There's a rhythm in this movement, a quiet dance between your body and the earth. Allow yourself to fully experience each part of the process. How do your muscles feel as they engage to lift your foot? What happens in your legs and hips as they move in unison?

Mindful walking invites you to be fully present in your body, to notice how it moves, to listen to its signals. If you find your mind wandering, gently bring it back to the sensations in your feet or the movement of your legs. There's no need to judge yourself for drifting—this is part of the practice. You are simply returning, again and again, to the present moment, to your body, to the earth beneath you.

As you walk, notice the connection between your breath and your movement. You might find that your breath naturally syncs with your steps, creating a sense of flow. Feel how the breath nourishes your body, giving you the energy to take another step. Each breath, each step, is a reminder that you are alive, that you are moving forward, that healing is happening, even in these small moments. There's no rush in this practice. In fact, slowing down is key—giving yourself permission to savor each step, each breath.

Mindful walking can be especially powerful in trauma recovery because trauma often disconnects us from our bodies. We may feel like strangers in our own skin, uncertain of how to inhabit ourselves fully. By bringing gentle awareness to the simple act of walking, we begin to reclaim that connection. Each step becomes an opportunity to ground ourselves, to feel the earth beneath us, and to remind our bodies that it's safe to be here. Walking in this way allows us to release stored tension, to let go of the tightness that trauma so often creates in our muscles and tissues. It's as though with each step, we shed a little more of the burden, making space for ease, for release, for healing.

There's something deeply comforting about knowing that the earth is always there, supporting you with every step. In mindful walking, you become aware of that relationship, the way your feet connect with the ground, the way the earth holds you up, no matter where you are on your journey. This practice helps you return to your body, to reclaim the simple joys of movement, and to restore a sense of connection that may have been lost in the wake of trauma. Through this gentle, mindful practice, you begin to build a bridge back to yourself, one step at a time.

Chapter 6

Navigating Triggers and Emotional Flashbacks

What Are Triggers and Why Do They Happen?

In the context of trauma recovery, triggers are experiences, sensations, or situations that bring back the emotional, physical, or mental pain associated with unresolved trauma. These triggers can be anything from a smell, a sound, a specific word, or even an environment that, on the surface, seems unrelated to the traumatic event itself. When trauma isn't fully processed, the body and mind store fragments of the experience, often in subtle, unexpected ways. This means that even seemingly harmless stimuli can set off a cascade of reactions, thrusting someone back into the emotional state they were in during the traumatic event.

Triggers arise because unresolved trauma often lingers beneath the surface, waiting to be activated by something that reminds the body or mind of the original experience. The brain is incredibly powerful at connecting dots, even when we aren't consciously aware of those links. For instance, if someone experienced a traumatic event during a thunderstorm, even the distant rumble of thunder may stir up a deep sense of dread. These triggers bypass the rational mind, pulling a person directly into their body's fight, flight, or freeze response. It's as if the body remembers the trauma before the brain can even catch up. This is why a trigger can lead to overwhelming emotions, flashbacks, or even physical symptoms like shaking, sweating, or a racing heart.

Flashbacks are one of the most common results of being triggered. In a flashback, a person can feel like they are reliving the traumatic event in real time. The sights, sounds, and sensations of the past may flood their awareness, making it difficult to distinguish between the past and the present. Even if the person intellectually knows they are safe, their body reacts as though they are in immediate danger. This overwhelming experience can be terrifying and leave someone feeling powerless. It's important to remember that this is the body's way of trying to protect itself, even though it feels anything but protective.

Physical reactions to triggers are also common. Some people might experience a tightness in their chest, a pounding heart, or trembling limbs. These reactions are signs that the body's nervous system is responding to a perceived threat, even if that threat isn't actually present in the moment. Triggers can also cause emotional overwhelm, leading to feelings of intense fear, anger, sadness, or panic. These emotions can come on suddenly, and they may seem out of proportion to the situation at hand, which can add to the confusion and distress someone might feel.

Common triggers can vary widely from person to person. A particular scent, like perfume or cigarette smoke, might remind someone of a traumatic moment. A loud noise, like fireworks or a slamming door, might suddenly make them feel like they're back in the thick of a violent situation. Even a certain time of year, a song, or the way someone speaks can act as a trigger. The key is that these triggers are deeply personal and often linked to sensory memories that the conscious mind may not fully recognize but the body vividly recalls.

It's important for readers to understand that these reactions are entirely normal. Triggers are not signs of weakness or failure but simply a reflection of how trauma has impacted the nervous system. The body is doing its best to protect itself, even if it doesn't always feel like that's what's happening in the moment. Everyone's triggers and responses will be unique, and recognizing them is the first step toward understanding how trauma continues to affect the mind and body, even long after the event itself has passed.

Identifying Your Personal Triggers

Understanding your personal triggers is one of the most empowering steps in your trauma recovery journey. It's like shining a light on the unseen forces that drive your emotions, allowing you to regain control of how you react to stress or distressing situations. Triggers can take many forms—certain places, people, smells, sounds, or even thoughts. They stir up past memories and emotions, often bringing feelings of anxiety or dread to the surface. The key to managing them lies in recognizing them, and that starts with noticing patterns in how your body and mind respond.

Start by paying attention to your emotional and physical reactions in various situations. When you feel a sudden wave of anxiety, sadness, or anger, pause for a moment and ask yourself: *What just happened?* It could be something as subtle as a certain tone of voice, the way a room is lit, or even a particular time of day. These may seem minor, but they can be powerful reminders of past trauma. Keep a small notebook or use an app on your phone to jot down moments when you notice these feelings arising. Write down as much detail as you can about the situation, including the physical sensations that came with it—did your heart race? Did your muscles tense? Did you feel a tightness in your chest or throat? These physical cues are often the first signs that your body is reacting to a trigger before your mind fully realizes it.

Now, let's take this awareness a step further by reflecting on these moments in a deeper way. Once you've logged a few experiences, set aside time in a quiet space where you can look back over your notes. As you read, ask yourself: *Are there any patterns here?* Do you notice that certain types of interactions or specific environments tend to spark these reactions? Perhaps loud noises or sudden changes in plans unsettle you. Or maybe certain smells or textures remind you of past experiences. These patterns are clues to your personal triggers, and recognizing them is the first step toward defusing their power over you.

In addition to recognizing patterns in your emotional responses, pay attention to your physical reactions. Your body often gives you information that your mind is too busy to notice. For instance, a sudden feeling of discomfort, a shift in your posture, or a desire to withdraw from a situation can be your body's way of alerting you to something that feels unsafe or overwhelming. Tuning into these signals can help you become more attuned to your triggers. When you feel these reactions, pause and check in with yourself: *What am I feeling in this moment? What might have just caused this sensation?* This process of self-inquiry can illuminate connections between your past experiences and your present emotional and physical state.

To help further identify your triggers, I encourage you to practice an exercise I like to call "body-mind mapping." Start by sitting in a quiet place and closing your eyes. Take a few deep breaths, allowing yourself to relax and settle into the present moment. As you breathe, bring your awareness to different parts of your body, starting from your head and moving down to your toes. Notice if any areas feel tight, tense, or uncomfortable. Now, think back to a recent moment when you felt triggered or anxious, and see if recalling that situation causes any physical changes. Does your chest tighten or your heart race? Does your body feel heavier or lighter? By mapping these sensations, you can begin to connect certain emotional responses with physical cues.

Tracking your emotional and physical responses over time is key to understanding your triggers. You might find it helpful to create a journal dedicated specifically to this purpose. Each day, write down situations that felt emotionally charged, how your body reacted, and any sensations or memories that surfaced. Over time, you'll start to see more clearly the situations, environments, or even types of interactions that are likely to provoke stress, anxiety, or flashbacks. The act of writing things down also helps externalize these experiences, making them feel more manageable and less overwhelming.

As you uncover these patterns, remember that this is not about self-judgment but about self-awareness. It's an ongoing process of learning to understand yourself better and to take back control from those hidden forces that may have felt uncontrollable for so long. By recognizing your triggers, you can start preparing for them—either by finding ways to avoid them when possible or developing strategies to manage your reactions when they arise. Keep reminding yourself that this is a journey, one where even small steps forward are significant and worth celebrating. You're learning to navigate your world with more awareness and strength each day.

Somatic Techniques for Managing Triggers

When it comes to managing emotional triggers and flashbacks, somatic techniques can be incredibly effective in helping you stay grounded and present in the moment. One powerful approach is grounding. This technique involves reconnecting with your body and the physical space around you, allowing you to anchor yourself in the present rather than getting swept away by overwhelming emotions. You might try a simple grounding exercise like the "5-4-3-2-1" technique. Begin by taking a deep breath, then take note of five things you can see, four things you can touch, three things you can hear, two things you can smell, and one thing you can taste. This sensory awareness helps you pull your attention away from distressing thoughts and brings you back to your surroundings.

Mindful breathing is another valuable tool in your somatic toolkit. It's amazing how something as simple as your breath can serve as a lifeline during intense moments. When you notice your anxiety rising or a flashback beginning, take a moment to focus on your breath. Inhale deeply through your nose, allowing your belly to expand, and then exhale slowly through your mouth. Try counting your breaths—inhale for a count of four, hold for four, and exhale for six. This rhythmic pattern not only calms your mind but also sends signals to your nervous system that it's safe to relax. By engaging in mindful breathing, you can create a sense of space between you and the emotional storm, helping to reduce the intensity of your trigger response.

Self-soothing exercises are another fantastic way to help you manage emotional triggers. Think of these techniques as your personal comfort toolkit. When you find yourself in distress, you might wrap a warm blanket around your shoulders, take a warm bath, or hold a comforting object—like a soft stuffed animal or a smooth stone. Engaging your senses in nurturing ways can create a sense of safety and reassurance. You could also practice gentle movements, such as stretching or swaying your body side to side, which can help release pent-up tension and promote relaxation.

Each of these techniques works to calm your nervous system by activating the parasympathetic response, which is your body's natural way of returning to a state of calm after stress. They encourage you to shift your focus from the fight-or-flight response—often triggered by memories of past trauma—to a more relaxed state, allowing you to regain control over your emotional experience. By incorporating grounding, mindful breathing, and self-soothing exercises into your daily routine, you're not just creating a toolbox for crisis moments; you're also fostering a deeper connection with your body and emotions. This ongoing practice can empower you to navigate the complexities of trauma recovery with greater ease and resilience.

Building Resilience Against Future Triggers

Building resilience is a fundamental aspect of trauma recovery, acting as a protective shield against the weight of past experiences and the potential impact of future triggers. When we talk about resilience, we're referring to the ability to bounce back from adversity, to adapt, and to keep moving forward despite the challenges we face. It's not about being unaffected by trauma; rather, it's about learning how to navigate its effects with greater ease and strength. This journey is deeply personal, often filled with ups and downs, but the path toward resilience is something every individual can cultivate with the right tools and mindset.

One of the most effective ways to strengthen resilience is through regular somatic practices. These practices focus on reconnecting the mind and body, allowing us to become more attuned to our physical sensations and emotional responses. Simple activities like yoga, tai chi, or even mindful walking can foster a sense of safety and stability within our bodies. By integrating these movements into our daily routines, we not only improve our physical health but also create a foundation of emotional resilience. When we feel grounded in our bodies, we are better equipped to handle stressors and triggers that may arise.

Mindfulness also plays a critical role in building resilience. It invites us to be present with our thoughts and feelings without judgment. When we practice mindfulness, we create space to acknowledge our experiences, allowing us to respond to stress with greater awareness and clarity. Techniques such as mindful breathing or body scans can help calm the nervous system and center our thoughts, making it easier to navigate moments of anxiety or overwhelm. The beauty of mindfulness is that it can be woven into our daily lives, transforming routine tasks into opportunities for self-discovery and healing.

In addition to somatic practices and mindfulness, self-care routines are essential for nurturing resilience. Prioritizing self-care means recognizing our own needs and actively seeking ways to fulfill them, whether that's through engaging in hobbies, spending time with loved ones, or simply allowing ourselves to rest. It's about creating a life that honors our well-being and fosters growth. By developing a self-care regimen, we equip ourselves with the tools to recharge and rejuvenate, ensuring we have the energy to face the challenges that life may throw our way.

Healing from trauma is rarely a straightforward journey; it's a gradual process that unfolds over time. Each step forward, no matter how small, contributes to our resilience. There may be moments of struggle and setbacks, but these are not signs of failure. Instead, they offer valuable lessons that teach us about our strengths and areas for growth. As we continue to engage in somatic practices, embrace mindfulness, and prioritize self-care, we gradually build a reservoir of resilience that not only helps us heal but also empowers us to thrive in the face of adversity.

This process of growth is like nurturing a garden; it takes patience and care, but the blooms of resilience can become a beautiful part of our lives, helping us navigate the complexities of our emotional landscape with grace and strength. As we learn to trust ourselves and our abilities, we become better equipped to handle future challenges, transforming our experiences into a source of wisdom and strength.

Chapter 7

Finding Support and Moving Forward

Healing from trauma is a deeply personal journey, but one thing remains clear: finding emotional, physical, and social support is essential. Trauma often creates a sense of isolation, making individuals feel like they're navigating a dark tunnel alone. It's not uncommon for those who have experienced trauma to withdraw from their friends, family, and even social activities they once enjoyed. This withdrawal can stem from feelings of shame, confusion, or the overwhelming weight of distress that trauma can bring. When you're in that state, the idea of reaching out for support may feel daunting, but it's precisely during these times that connection becomes crucial.

Imagine having a safety net of people who understand or are willing to listen to your struggles. A support network can be made up of friends who lend a compassionate ear, family members who offer understanding, or professionals trained to help navigate the complexities of trauma recovery. Each person in your support system plays a unique role, providing different perspectives and strengths that can help you find your way back to a sense of safety and security. Friends may bring lightness to your days, while family members can ground you with familiarity. Professionals can offer tools and strategies that you may not have considered on your own. Together, they can help you weave a fabric of support that catches you when you stumble and lifts you when you feel low.

In many ways, having a support network acts as a mirror reflecting back your worth and resilience. When trauma makes you doubt yourself, the encouragement and validation from others can reignite your sense of self. Sharing your experiences with trusted individuals can lighten the emotional load, transforming heavy burdens into shared journeys. This connection also fosters an environment where vulnerability is embraced rather than shunned, allowing you to explore your feelings without judgment.

Moreover, social support provides practical benefits, too. Just knowing there's someone to call when things feel overwhelming can instill a sense of security. It can encourage you to engage in self-care activities, attend therapy, or participate in healing practices you might otherwise shy away from. The presence of supportive friends and family can motivate you to take those necessary steps toward recovery.

Ultimately, the journey to healing doesn't have to be solitary. Reaching out to create or strengthen your support network is a courageous act that signals your commitment to reclaiming your life. It's a reminder that while trauma may have shaken your foundation, the connections you cultivate can serve as solid ground on which to rebuild. Embrace this process, allowing yourself the grace to lean on others as you forge your path toward healing and wholeness.

Choosing the Right Somatic Therapist

Finding the right somatic therapist can feel like a daunting task, especially when you're navigating the complex emotions that come with trauma recovery. It's essential to choose someone who not only understands the nuances of somatic therapy but also resonates with your unique experiences and needs. The journey begins with understanding the qualities that make for an effective and compassionate therapist.

One of the first things to consider is their level of experience, particularly in working with trauma. You'll want someone who has a solid foundation in both somatic therapy and trauma-informed care. Look for a therapist who has undergone specific training in these areas and has a background that reflects a commitment to helping individuals heal from trauma. A good therapist should be able to articulate their approach and share how they integrate somatic techniques into their practice. This not only gives you confidence in their expertise but also helps you understand what to expect from your sessions.

Compassion is another vital quality to look for. A therapist should create a safe and welcoming environment where you feel free to express your feelings without fear of judgment. You might sense this compassion in their demeanor—how they listen, how they respond, and how they hold space for your emotions. It's helpful to choose a therapist who is attuned to the subtle cues of your body language and emotional state, as this sensitivity can foster a deeper sense of connection and trust.

As you start your search, consider reaching out to potential therapists for an initial consultation or phone call. This can be a great opportunity to gauge how you feel in their presence. Do they make you feel heard and understood? Do they take the time to explore your specific needs and experiences? This interaction can often provide insight into whether they are the right fit for you. It's important to remember that you should feel a sense of ease and safety when communicating with them.

In sessions, you can expect a blend of conversation and experiential exercises. A skilled somatic therapist will guide you through body awareness practices, helping you connect physical sensations with emotional experiences. They might incorporate gentle movement, breathwork, or mindfulness techniques to assist you in releasing tension and trauma stored in your body. Be open to the experience, but also trust your instincts. If something feels uncomfortable or misaligned with your healing process, a good therapist will encourage you to voice those feelings.

Ultimately, assessing whether a therapist is a good fit for you is about feeling respected and validated throughout the process. Pay attention to how you feel after your sessions. Do you leave feeling more connected to your body and emotions? Are you learning to navigate your triggers with greater awareness? Healing is a deeply personal journey, and the right somatic therapist will empower you to reclaim your sense of safety and agency. Remember, it's perfectly okay to try out different therapists until you find someone who feels like the right match for you—your healing deserves that kind of dedication.

Creating a Personal Healing Plan

Creating a personalized healing plan is a powerful step in your journey toward recovery, one that honors your unique needs and aspirations. Think of this plan as a roadmap—a flexible guide that can adapt as you grow and learn more about yourself. Start by reflecting on your individual experiences and how they shape your healing journey. What specific challenges are you facing? Are there particular triggers that arise in your daily life? Acknowledging these aspects is crucial, as it helps you identify where to focus your energy and attention.

Once you have a clearer picture of your challenges, it's time to think about your goals. Setting realistic and achievable goals can make a significant difference in your recovery process. Instead of overwhelming yourself with lofty ambitions, consider what small, manageable steps you can take. For instance, if anxiety often creeps in during the day, a goal might be to practice mindful breathing for just five minutes each morning. Or, if you're looking to reconnect with your body, you might aim to incorporate gentle stretching or movement into your routine a few times a week. Remember, these goals should be tailored to you—what feels meaningful and attainable in your life?

Next, let's integrate somatic practices into your daily routine. This is where the magic happens. Begin by choosing a few somatic techniques that resonate with you—whether it's mindful breathing, gentle movement, or grounding exercises. Consider setting aside specific times in your day to engage in these practices, creating a sense of consistency and ritual. For example, you might dedicate a few minutes in the morning to check in with your body, noticing any tension or discomfort, and then follow that with some mindful breathing. You could also establish a calming bedtime routine that includes gentle stretches or a body scan to promote relaxation and ease into sleep.

In addition to personal practices, think about the role of professional support in your healing journey. Connecting with a somatic therapist or counselor can provide invaluable guidance as you navigate the complexities of trauma recovery. If you feel comfortable, include a goal to explore therapy options or join a support group where you can share experiences with others who understand your journey. This connection can foster a sense of community and help you feel less isolated in your experiences.

As you weave together your goals, practices, and support systems, it's essential to remain flexible. Your healing plan is not set in stone; it's a living document that can change as you progress. Regularly check in with yourself—how are the practices feeling? Are your goals still aligned with where you are on your journey? Adjusting your plan as needed ensures that it remains a true reflection of your needs and growth.

Throughout this process, celebrate your wins, no matter how small. Each step you take, whether it's a new practice, a breakthrough in understanding, or simply a day where you feel a bit lighter, is worthy of acknowledgment. Remember, healing is not linear; it has its ebbs and flows, and that's completely okay. You are building resilience and learning to navigate life with a new sense of awareness and empowerment. Embrace this journey with compassion, and trust that every effort you make is a step toward reclaiming your body and restoring your life.

The Journey of Healing: What to Expect Moving Forward

Healing from trauma is a journey that can often feel like a winding path, filled with both ups and downs. It's essential to understand from the outset that recovery is not a straight line; rather, it resembles a series of peaks and valleys. There will be days when you feel empowered, full of hope and resilience, ready to face the world with renewed strength. On other days, you might find yourself grappling with overwhelming emotions, perhaps feeling as though you've taken several steps back. This ebb and flow is entirely normal, and it doesn't mean you're failing; it's simply a part of the healing process.

As you embark on this journey, remember that it's perfectly okay to have mixed feelings about your progress. There may be moments of frustration when the memories resurface or when stressors in life feel particularly challenging. Acknowledge these feelings without judgment; they are valid and part of your experience. It's crucial to approach these fluctuations with kindness toward yourself. Celebrate the small victories along the way, whether that's successfully using a grounding technique in a stressful moment or simply allowing yourself to rest when you need it. Each step forward, no matter how small, is a testament to your strength and determination.

Moreover, healing is a process that unfolds at its own pace. There might be times when you feel stuck, as if progress has stalled. During these periods, it's important to revisit the tools and practices you've learned. Engaging with somatic exercises, breathing techniques, or gentle movements can help shift your energy and encourage emotional release. Remember that every bit of work you put into your healing—every deep breath, every moment of awareness—is nurturing your growth and transformation.

As you continue to explore somatic therapy, you may notice deeper connections forming within yourself. You're not just healing; you're evolving. With each practice, you're learning more about your body's wisdom and your emotional landscape. You're developing a heightened sense of self-awareness that will serve you well beyond the realm of trauma recovery. Embrace this journey of self-discovery. Recognize that your experiences, both challenging and uplifting, are shaping you into a stronger, more resilient person.

Healing is also a journey of reconnecting with joy and hope. As you progress, you might find that activities you once enjoyed return to your life, or that you're more open to new experiences. This reawakening is a beautiful aspect of the recovery process. Embrace the moments of joy and connection as they arise. They are reminders that healing is not just about overcoming pain; it's also about rediscovering the richness of life and the beauty that exists in each day.

So, as you continue this journey, be gentle with yourself. Remember that it's perfectly okay to feel a range of emotions and to have days that are harder than others. Each moment you dedicate to your healing is a step toward reclaiming your life. You are not alone in this process, and you are stronger than you know. Every effort you make, no matter how small, is a step toward a future filled with hope, empowerment, and the possibility of a more peaceful existence. Trust in the journey, and allow yourself the grace to navigate it at your own pace.

Chapter 8

Building Resilience Through Somatic Practices

Resilience, in the context of trauma recovery, can be understood as the capacity to adapt and bounce back in the face of adversity. It's that remarkable quality that enables individuals to endure the emotional and psychological strains that trauma often brings, allowing them to regain a sense of balance and well-being. This resilience is not just a psychological phenomenon; it encompasses physiological responses as well. When faced with challenges, our bodies instinctively mobilize resources to cope. This includes activating stress response systems, releasing hormones, and prompting physical changes that help us survive difficult situations. Yet, while these mechanisms are hardwired into our biology, resilience isn't just about how our bodies respond; it's also about how we think, feel, and engage with the world around us.

Every individual possesses resilience, even if they don't always recognize it. This inherent strength is part of our human makeup. From the moment we are born, we are equipped with survival instincts and the capacity to learn from our experiences. Think of a child learning to walk. They stumble and fall countless times, but each time, they get back up, driven by an instinctual desire to explore and move forward. This simple yet profound example illustrates that resilience isn't just reserved for monumental events; it's a thread woven through the fabric of our everyday lives.

In the face of trauma, resilience can manifest in various ways. Psychologically, it might show up as a person choosing to seek therapy after experiencing loss or abuse, recognizing that support is essential for healing. Physiologically, resilience can be seen when individuals engage in self-care practices, such as exercise, meditation, or simply taking time to breathe deeply. These actions foster both mental and physical health, allowing the body to recover from stress and trauma. For instance, someone may find solace in nature, taking regular walks in the park to clear their mind and rejuvenate their spirit.

Reflecting on our personal experiences of overcoming challenges can illuminate our innate resilience. Perhaps you remember a time when life felt particularly heavy, yet you found the strength to navigate through it. Maybe you leaned on friends or family, or perhaps you discovered a new passion that reignited your zest for life. These moments of perseverance, however small they may seem, are proof of your resilience. Each step taken toward healing is a testament to your strength, illustrating that even in the darkest of times, a light can be found within.

As you read this, take a moment to think about your own life. Can you recall instances where you faced adversity but chose to move forward? What strategies did you employ, consciously or unconsciously, to help you cope? Reflecting on these experiences can serve as a reminder that resilience is not only a potential within you but also a powerful force that has carried you through tough times before. Embracing this perspective can be a transformative step in your journey of healing, helping you to recognize that, like a phoenix, you too can rise from the ashes of trauma, stronger and more vibrant than ever.

Somatic Practices to Cultivate Strength and Flexibility

Cultivating mental strength and physical flexibility is a transformative journey that can profoundly impact how we respond to stress and navigate life's challenges. Somatic practices, which focus on the mind-body connection, are essential tools in this journey. They invite us to explore gentle movements, stretching, and breathwork, all of which can foster resilience and adaptability.

Gentle movement is a wonderful way to tune into our bodies and release stored tension. Activities like yoga, tai chi, or simply walking mindfully can help us cultivate a sense of presence. Imagine moving through a series of slow, deliberate poses, where each transition feels fluid and natural. This not only enhances our physical flexibility but also encourages mental awareness. When we move with intention, we learn to recognize where we hold stress, allowing us to address those areas consciously. Research supports this, showing that gentle movement can activate the parasympathetic nervous system, promoting relaxation and reducing anxiety.

Stretching is another powerful somatic practice that enhances both physical flexibility and mental resilience. When we engage in regular stretching, we open up our muscles and joints, relieving tightness that often accompanies stress. Think of a simple neck stretch, where you tilt your head gently from side to side, feeling the release of tension with each breath. This not only increases our physical range of motion but also fosters a sense of ease and comfort within our bodies. The science behind stretching shows that it increases blood flow and oxygen to our muscles, which can enhance our mood and cognitive function. By integrating stretching into our daily routine, we cultivate a mindset of openness and adaptability.

Breathwork, perhaps one of the most accessible and powerful somatic practices, allows us to tap into our body's innate ability to self-regulate. Through conscious breathing techniques—like diaphragmatic breathing or box breathing—we can effectively manage our stress response. Picture yourself taking a deep breath, feeling your abdomen rise as you inhale, then gently releasing the breath, letting go of tension. This practice calms the nervous system and provides clarity of thought, empowering us to respond to stressors with greater composure. The science behind breathwork reveals that controlled breathing can lower cortisol levels, reduce anxiety, and improve emotional regulation, making it a cornerstone of resilience.

Engaging in these somatic practices offers a holistic approach to building strength and flexibility. As we cultivate awareness through gentle movements, relieve tension through stretching, and regulate our emotions through breathwork, we are not just working on our physical bodies; we are nurturing our mental fortitude. This interconnectedness is the essence of somatic therapy. It teaches us that our experiences are not solely mental or physical but a beautiful blend of both, encouraging us to embrace each moment with greater adaptability and resilience.

Creating a Daily Practice to Support Your Well-Being

Creating a personalized daily practice that incorporates somatic techniques can be a transformative way to enhance your well-being and support your healing journey. The key to developing a routine that resonates with you lies in understanding your own needs, preferences, and lifestyle. Start by setting aside a few moments each day dedicated solely to these practices, treating them as sacred time for yourself. Whether it's early in the morning, during a lunch break, or before bedtime, find a slot that feels right and stick to it consistently. Regularity is what builds momentum, so aim for short, manageable sessions that fit seamlessly into your day.

Consider beginning with gentle movement exercises, focusing on flexibility and strength-building. You might incorporate a series of stretches that target areas where you often feel tension, like your neck, shoulders, and lower back. Just five to ten minutes of stretching can help release tightness and bring awareness to your body. As you become more comfortable, you can gradually extend this practice, adding in yoga poses or light strength exercises that engage major muscle groups. Even simple movements, like squats or lunges, can help you build strength while promoting a sense of grounding and connection with your body. Listen to what feels good; if an exercise doesn't resonate with you, feel free to explore alternatives that do.

In addition to physical movement, integrating mindfulness practices into your daily routine can greatly enhance your somatic experience. Consider starting or ending your day with a few minutes of mindful breathing. This could involve focusing on the sensation of your breath flowing in and out, noticing how your chest rises and falls. Pairing this with visualization— imagining your breath as a wave washing over you— can deepen your connection to the present moment. Throughout your day, take opportunities to check in with your body, pausing to notice areas of tension or discomfort. A simple, mindful scan of your body can remind you to return to a more relaxed state.

Another effective approach is to incorporate grounding exercises. You can practice these whenever you feel overwhelmed or disconnected. Try standing firmly on the ground, feeling the weight of your body pressing down into the earth. You might even close your eyes and take several slow, deep breaths, allowing each inhale to fill your lungs and each exhale to release any built-up tension. If it helps, visualize roots extending from your feet into the ground, anchoring you in the present moment and creating a sense of stability.

Consistency is vital. To foster this, consider creating a chart or journal where you can track your daily practices. Note how you feel before and after each session; this reflection can be incredibly motivating as you begin to see the cumulative benefits of your efforts. Remember, this is your journey, so give yourself permission to be flexible with your routine. If one day you feel drawn to more movement, embrace it; on another, a quieter, reflective practice may call to you. This adaptability allows your practice to grow alongside your evolving needs.

Engaging in a mix of somatic techniques—flexibility exercises, strength-building, mindful breathing, and grounding—can create a holistic daily routine that nurtures both your body and mind. It's about cultivating a sense of harmony and connection, enhancing your overall well-being in a way that feels authentic and supportive. As you embark on this journey, remind yourself that every small step counts and contributes to your greater healing process. Celebrate your commitment to yourself, knowing that consistency and compassion will guide you toward a more balanced, empowered life.

Integrating Somatic Techniques into Everyday Life

Integrating somatic techniques into your daily routine can be a transformative way to enhance your overall well-being and create a deeper connection with your body. It's all about weaving mindfulness and awareness into the fabric of your everyday life, allowing these practices to naturally flow into the moments that make up your day. Imagine starting your morning with a gentle stretch. As you rise from bed, take a moment to stretch your arms overhead, feeling the lengthening of your spine and the gentle awakening of your muscles. This simple act of awareness not only helps shake off sleepiness but also sets a mindful tone for the day ahead.

When you step outside for a walk, try to embrace the experience with a sense of curiosity. Pay attention to the sensations in your feet as they connect with the ground, feeling the earth beneath you. With each step, you can practice mindful breathing—taking a deep breath in as you step forward and gently releasing it as you bring your foot down. This rhythmic connection between your breath and movement not only calms the nervous system but also anchors you in the present moment. Notice the sights, sounds, and even the smells around you. Allow these sensory experiences to enrich your walk, making it more than just a means of getting from point A to point B.

Sitting at your desk doesn't have to be a mindless activity; it can become an opportunity for somatic awareness. As you work, take periodic breaks to check in with your body. Notice any areas of tension, especially in your shoulders or lower back, which often hold stress. Stand up and take a moment to stretch gently, rolling your shoulders back and taking a few mindful breaths. You might even incorporate a simple seated stretch, where you reach one arm overhead and lean to the opposite side, feeling the delightful stretch along your side. This not only refreshes your body but also revitalizes your mind, allowing you to return to your tasks with renewed focus.

Even during stressful moments, you can bring somatic practices into play. When you feel tension building—whether it's from a demanding project or an unexpected challenge—pause for a moment. Close your eyes if you can and take a few deep, deliberate breaths. Inhale slowly through your nose, filling your belly with air, and then exhale gently through your mouth, imagining the stress leaving your body with each breath. You can also place a hand on your heart or belly, feeling the rise and fall as you breathe. This simple act of grounding yourself can help re-center your thoughts and emotions, transforming a moment of stress into an opportunity for calm.

Incorporating gentle movements throughout your day is another wonderful way to embrace somatic techniques. If you're waiting for a meeting to start or taking a brief break, try a few gentle neck rolls or wrist stretches. These small actions can significantly ease tension and enhance your body's awareness. If you have a moment of solitude, consider trying a few simple yoga poses. Even a few minutes of downward dog or cat-cow stretches can awaken your body and relieve built-up stress.

Ultimately, the beauty of somatic practices lies in their flexibility and adaptability. You don't have to set aside large chunks of time to practice; rather, you can seamlessly integrate these techniques into your daily life. Each small moment you take to check in with your body, breathe mindfully, or move gently adds up, creating a profound impact on your overall sense of well-being. Embrace these practices as not just exercises but as invitations to enhance your everyday experiences, turning mundane moments into opportunities for connection, healing, and joy.

Chapter 9

Dealing with Stress and Anxiety: Your Somatic Toolkit

When we talk about the body's stress response, we're diving into a fascinating and intricate system that has evolved to help us survive. Imagine a time in your life when you faced a sudden threat—maybe it was a near-miss while driving or a surprising encounter with an aggressive dog. In moments like these, your body springs into action, preparing you to either fight or flee. This is known as the fight-or-flight response, a term that captures the essence of how our bodies instinctively react to danger.

Physiologically, when a perceived threat arises, your brain quickly processes the situation. The amygdala, a small almond-shaped structure in the brain, detects the danger and sends a signal to the hypothalamus, which is like your body's command center. This leads to the activation of the sympathetic nervous system, triggering the adrenal glands to release stress hormones such as adrenaline and cortisol. These hormones flood your system, increasing your heart rate, boosting your energy levels, and heightening your awareness. You might notice your breathing becoming faster, your muscles tensing, and your senses sharpening—all preparing you to either confront the danger or escape from it.

While this response is life-saving in moments of immediate threat, it can become problematic when it's triggered too frequently or for prolonged periods. Trauma, whether from a single incident like an accident or from ongoing experiences such as abuse or neglect, can alter how our bodies respond to stress. For someone who has experienced trauma, the body may start to misinterpret ordinary situations as threats, leading to an exaggerated stress response even in safe environments. This means that everyday stressors—like a busy workday or a disagreement with a loved one—can trigger that same fight-or-flight reaction, putting the body on high alert.

Imagine going into a meeting feeling anxious, your heart racing and palms sweating. This heightened state of alertness may be your body's way of preparing for a perceived threat, even if there's no real danger present. Over time, this can lead to chronic stress, where your body remains in a constant state of tension, ready to react. This state of chronic stress can contribute to various health issues, including anxiety disorders, digestive problems, and even heart disease.

Recognizing your own stress responses is crucial in navigating the challenges of life, especially if you have a history of trauma. It's essential to tune into how your body feels in different situations. Do you find your muscles tightening when you're stressed? Does your mind race, making it hard to focus? Understanding these signals is the first step toward finding ways to manage stress effectively.

As you start to identify your stress responses, remember that you're not alone. Many people experience similar reactions, especially those who have faced difficult experiences. By acknowledging how your body reacts to stress, you empower yourself to take control and find healthier ways to cope. Instead of being at the mercy of your body's automatic responses, you can learn techniques to soothe and calm yourself, bringing balance back into your life.

Your Somatic Toolkit: Quick Techniques to Ease Anxiety

When anxiety hits, having a toolkit of somatic techniques at your fingertips can make all the difference. Let's explore some quick and effective strategies that you can use in those moments of distress, empowering you to reclaim a sense of calm and safety within your body.

One of the most effective ways to ground yourself is through a simple grounding exercise. Start by finding a comfortable position, whether sitting or standing. Take a moment to notice the sensations in your feet. Feel the weight of your body pressing down into the ground, and visualize roots extending from your feet deep into the earth, anchoring you firmly. As you breathe in, imagine drawing up strength and stability from the ground below, and as you exhale, release any tension or unease. You can even use your senses to deepen this practice: take a moment to notice five things you can see around you, four things you can touch, three things you can hear, two things you can smell, and one thing you can taste. This exercise not only helps you stay present but also reconnects you to your physical environment, allowing anxiety to dissipate.

Deep breathing is another powerful tool in your somatic toolkit. When anxiety strikes, your breath often becomes shallow and quick, which can exacerbate feelings of panic. To counter this, try a technique called diaphragmatic breathing. Start by sitting comfortably or lying down, placing one hand on your belly and the other on your chest. Inhale deeply through your nose, allowing your belly to expand fully, while keeping your chest relatively still. Feel the air filling your lower lungs, and hold for a moment. Then, exhale slowly through your mouth, letting your belly fall. Aim for a ratio of four counts in, a brief pause, and then six counts out. This extended exhalation activates your parasympathetic nervous system, which helps to calm the body and reduce anxiety. Practice this for a few minutes, focusing solely on the rhythm of your breath, and you'll likely notice a shift in your physical and emotional state.

Gentle stretches can also be an excellent way to release built-up tension and promote relaxation. One simple stretch you can try is the neck roll. Sit or stand comfortably and take a deep breath in. As you exhale, gently drop your right ear toward your right shoulder, feeling a stretch along the left side of your neck. Hold this position for a few breaths, allowing your body to relax further with each exhale. Slowly roll your head forward and to the left, bringing your left ear toward your left shoulder. Hold, breathe, and then return to center. This gentle movement not only alleviates tension in the neck and shoulders but also encourages mindfulness and awareness of your body, drawing your attention away from anxious thoughts.

If you're looking for a quick movement to release anxiety, consider incorporating a few shoulder rolls. While seated or standing, inhale deeply and lift your shoulders up toward your ears. Hold for a moment, and then exhale forcefully as you roll your shoulders back and down. Repeat this motion several times, synchronizing your breath with the movement. This simple exercise helps release pent-up tension in your shoulders and upper back, areas that often hold stress. As you perform this movement, visualize the stress leaving your body with each exhale, creating space for calmness and clarity.

Finally, practicing mindfulness through a sensory awareness exercise can help you connect with the present moment and quiet racing thoughts. Take a few moments to engage your senses. Look around you and choose an object that catches your eye. It could be a plant, a piece of furniture, or even a pattern on the wall. Focus on this object, noticing its colors, shapes, and textures. If it's safe to do so, touch the object and observe how it feels against your skin. Pay attention to any sounds you hear in the background, perhaps the rustle of leaves outside or the hum of appliances. Allow yourself to immerse fully in this experience, and notice how it shifts your focus away from anxiety and into the present moment.

These somatic techniques are designed to be quick and easily integrated into your daily life. The key is to practice them regularly so that when anxiety arises, you can tap into these tools with ease and confidence. By embracing these practices, you're not just managing anxiety; you're building a deeper connection with your body, fostering resilience and strength as you navigate your journey to healing.

How to Calm Yourself Before, During, and After a Panic Attack

Managing panic attacks can be a daunting journey, but with the right strategies, you can find your way through these overwhelming experiences. Let's explore various approaches for managing panic attacks, focusing on prevention, calming techniques during an attack, and reflective exercises for processing the experience afterward. Throughout this journey, remember to practice self-compassion and stay attuned to your triggers.

Before a panic attack occurs, the best approach is to arm yourself with preventive techniques that foster resilience. Establishing a self-care routine is crucial. Regular exercise, even if it's just a daily walk, can significantly help reduce anxiety levels and improve your overall well-being. It's not just about physical fitness; movement releases endorphins that can elevate your mood and decrease feelings of tension. Moreover, consider incorporating mindfulness practices into your routine. Engaging in meditation, yoga, or deep breathing exercises regularly can cultivate a sense of calm and awareness that makes it easier to handle stress when it arises. When you take time each day to connect with your breath or focus on the present moment, you're essentially training your mind to remain grounded, even when anxiety threatens to pull you away.

Understanding your triggers is another essential preventive measure. Keep a journal to track when panic attacks occur and what might have preceded them. This can help you identify patterns or specific situations that lead to these episodes, enabling you to develop strategies for managing those triggers. For instance, if crowded places tend to spark anxiety, you might decide to avoid them when possible or prepare yourself with calming techniques in advance. Engaging in therapy, especially cognitive-behavioral therapy, can be invaluable. A therapist can work with you to develop personalized coping strategies tailored to your unique triggers and circumstances.

When a panic attack does strike, it can feel as though the world is closing in on you, but there are calming practices you can employ to help navigate the storm. One effective technique is to focus on your breath. When you feel that familiar rush of panic, take a moment to close your eyes and breathe deeply. Inhale slowly through your nose, allowing your abdomen to expand fully, and then exhale gently through your mouth. This simple act of breathing can help regulate your nervous system and signal to your body that it's okay to relax. Visualizing a peaceful scene or a safe space while you breathe can enhance this calming effect. Imagine yourself in a serene forest or lying on a warm beach; let the sensations of that place wash over you as you breathe deeply.

Grounding techniques can also be immensely helpful during an attack. Try focusing on the physical sensations in your body. Press your feet firmly into the ground, feeling the earth beneath you. Notice the weight of your body against the chair or floor, anchoring yourself to the present moment. You can also engage your senses by identifying five things you can see, four you can touch, three you can hear, two you can smell, and one you can taste. This technique redirects your focus from the panic to your surroundings, helping to create a sense of safety and stability.

Once the panic attack has subsided, it's important to take time to reflect on the experience and process what happened. This is where self-compassion truly comes into play. Acknowledge that you've just faced something difficult and that it's perfectly okay to feel shaken. Write in your journal about the experience, exploring what triggered the attack and how you responded. Be gentle with yourself as you do this. It's crucial to recognize that you are not defined by your panic; rather, you are a resilient individual navigating a challenging aspect of life.

Consider incorporating reflective exercises such as a "feelings wheel" to help you articulate the emotions that surfaced during the attack. By identifying your feelings, you gain clarity on what happened and how it affected you. This not only helps in understanding your emotional responses but also provides insight into how to cope better in the future. You might also want to list out your coping strategies that worked during the attack and those that didn't. Reflecting on this can be a powerful way to refine your approach, turning the experience into a learning opportunity for growth.

By embracing these strategies—preventive techniques before an attack, calming practices during an episode, and reflective exercises afterward—you create a supportive framework for managing panic attacks. Remember, you're not alone in this, and with time and practice, you can cultivate a greater sense of control and peace within yourself.

Finding Your Own Somatic Rhythm: What Works for You?

As you embark on your journey of trauma recovery, it's essential to explore a variety of somatic techniques to find what resonates with you personally. Each individual's experience with trauma is unique, and the path to healing can take many forms. By experimenting with different practices—such as breathwork, gentle movement, and grounding exercises—you can discover which methods align with your body's needs and preferences. This exploration is not just about finding what feels good; it's about tuning in to your body's wisdom and honoring its signals.

Breathwork, for example, can be a powerful tool for regulating your emotions and calming your nervous system. You might try simple techniques like deep diaphragmatic breathing or box breathing, where you inhale deeply for a count of four, hold for four, exhale for four, and pause for four before inhaling again. This rhythmic approach can ground you in the moment and help you reconnect with your body. As you practice, pay attention to how different breathing patterns affect your feelings of anxiety or stress. Notice any shifts in your body or mood as you engage in these exercises, allowing the breath to guide you toward a greater sense of calm.

Movement is another integral aspect of somatic therapy that can help release tension and stored emotions. You might explore gentle stretching or somatic yoga, focusing on slow, mindful movements that encourage awareness of your body's sensations. Dance, walking, or simply swaying can also be liberating. The key is to move in ways that feel good to you, letting your body lead the way. As you engage in these movements, check in with yourself. Are there areas of tightness or discomfort? How does your body respond to each movement? Allowing yourself the freedom to experiment with different forms of movement can unlock pathways to healing that you may not have previously recognized.

Grounding exercises can serve as an anchor during moments of overwhelm. Simple practices like focusing on the sensation of your feet on the ground or holding a comforting object can help you stay present and connected. You might also try the '5-4-3-2-1' technique, where you identify five things you can see, four things you can touch, three things you can hear, two things you can smell, and one thing you can taste. This exercise can effectively bring you back to the here and now, allowing you to regain a sense of safety within your body. As you practice these grounding techniques, notice how they affect your feelings of stability and security.

It's also vital to track your experiences as you explore these different practices. Keeping a journal can be an invaluable tool for reflection. Write down your thoughts and feelings before and after each session. How did each technique impact your emotional state? Did you feel more connected to your body? Did certain exercises evoke specific memories or sensations? By documenting your journey, you create a roadmap of your healing process, allowing you to see patterns and progress over time.

Remember, personalization is at the heart of this journey. What works for one person might not resonate with another, and that's perfectly okay. Listen to your body; it holds the key to what you need. If a particular technique feels uncomfortable or unhelpful, don't hesitate to set it aside and try something different. Healing is not a one-size-fits-all process; it's about finding the rhythm that suits you best. Embrace the journey with curiosity and compassion, allowing yourself the freedom to explore and adapt as you move forward in your healing.

Chapter 10

The Role of Mindfulness and Meditation in Somatic Healing

Mindfulness, in the context of somatic healing, is the practice of bringing one's attention to the present moment with a gentle, non-judgmental awareness of thoughts, feelings, and bodily sensations. It invites us to tune into our inner experiences without rushing to label or change them. This quality of presence is particularly crucial in trauma recovery, where past experiences can often resurface as physical tension, anxiety, or emotional distress. By cultivating mindfulness, we learn to reconnect with our bodies and our sensations, allowing us to navigate the complex landscape of trauma with greater compassion and understanding.

One of the key benefits of mindfulness for trauma recovery lies in its ability to create a safe space for us to experience discomfort without becoming overwhelmed. When we practice being present, we start to notice the ways our bodies respond to stress—perhaps a tightness in the chest or a fluttering in the stomach. Instead of getting swept away by these sensations or avoiding them altogether, mindfulness encourages us to observe them with curiosity. This process helps to desensitize us to triggers and reduces the intensity of our reactions over time. As we grow more aware of our bodily sensations, we can begin to separate them from the narratives we hold about our trauma, fostering a sense of agency and empowerment.

To weave mindfulness into our everyday lives, we can begin with small, manageable practices that ground us in the present. Start by setting aside a few minutes each day to engage in a mindful breathing exercise. Find a comfortable seated position, close your eyes, and focus on your breath. Inhale deeply through your nose, allowing your abdomen to expand fully. Then, exhale slowly through your mouth, feeling the release of air. As you breathe, pay attention to the sensations of your breath—the coolness of the air entering your nostrils, the warmth of your breath as it leaves your body. If your mind starts to wander, gently guide your focus back to your breath without judgment. This simple practice not only calms the nervous system but also helps anchor you in the present moment.

You can also integrate mindfulness into daily routines, such as when you're eating or walking. During meals, take a moment to appreciate the colors, textures, and aromas of your food. Chew slowly and savor each bite, paying attention to the flavors and sensations in your mouth. This practice not only enhances your enjoyment of food but also helps you connect with your body's hunger and fullness cues, fostering a more intuitive relationship with nourishment.

Mindful walking is another wonderful way to cultivate presence and awareness in your body. As you walk, notice the sensation of your feet making contact with the ground. Feel the weight shifting from one foot to the other, and become aware of the rhythm of your breath as you move. You might find it helpful to count your steps or synchronize your breath with your movement—inhale for three steps, then exhale for three steps. This not only centers you in your body but also transforms a simple walk into a nourishing practice of self-awareness.

Additionally, incorporating body scans into your mindfulness practice can deepen your connection to bodily sensations. Find a quiet space to lie down or sit comfortably, and close your eyes. Begin by taking a few deep breaths, allowing your body to relax with each exhale. Then, starting from the tips of your toes, slowly bring your awareness to each part of your body, moving upwards. Notice any areas of tension or discomfort without judgment, simply acknowledging their presence. As you move through your body, visualize breathing into those areas, inviting relaxation and ease. This practice can serve as a powerful tool to release stored tension and foster a greater sense of embodiment.

In each of these practices, remember that mindfulness is about acceptance and curiosity. It's not about achieving a particular state or forcing a change; rather, it's about being with what is, allowing yourself to experience the fullness of your sensations and emotions without getting swept away by them. By integrating mindfulness into your daily life, you cultivate a deeper connection with your body, fostering healing and resilience as you navigate the path of trauma recovery.

Meditation Techniques to Support Somatic Healing

Meditation can be a powerful ally in your journey through somatic therapy, offering you additional tools to deepen your connection between body and mind. By integrating various meditation techniques into your practice, you can create a rich tapestry of healing experiences that foster self-awareness, relaxation, and emotional resilience.

Guided meditations are a wonderful way to explore your inner landscape with the support of a soothing voice leading you through the experience. These sessions can be found in numerous formats, from apps to online videos, making it easy to find one that resonates with you. Imagine settling into a comfortable position, perhaps lying down or sitting in a cozy chair, and allowing the voice to gently guide you. As you listen, you might visualize a serene place, a garden, or a peaceful beach, where you feel safe and at ease. The guide may invite you to focus on your breath, encouraging you to inhale deeply and exhale slowly, releasing any tension that has built up in your body. With each breath, you may find yourself sinking deeper into relaxation, creating space for healing and connection within.

Another invaluable practice is the body scan meditation, which invites you to cultivate a profound awareness of your physical sensations. In this meditation, you'll begin by finding a quiet place where you won't be disturbed. As you close your eyes and take a few deep breaths, focus your attention on your body, starting from the tips of your toes and moving slowly upward. Imagine bringing your awareness to each area, noticing any sensations—warmth, tension, or perhaps a sense of lightness. This gentle exploration encourages you to be present with your body, acknowledging areas that may be holding onto stress or discomfort. With each scan, you can consciously release tension, breathe into tight spots, and embrace a sense of relaxation. This practice not only fosters connection between your body and mind but also allows you to develop a compassionate relationship with yourself.

Visualization is another dynamic technique that can enhance your somatic therapy practice. This method involves using your imagination to create vivid mental images that promote relaxation and healing. Picture a bright, golden light enveloping your entire body, bringing warmth and comfort to every cell. As you visualize this light, imagine it dissolving any stress or pain, replacing it with a soothing sense of calm. You might choose to visualize a protective barrier around you, keeping negativity at bay, or imagine your body moving freely and easily, reflecting the vitality you desire. Engaging your imagination in this way not only enriches your meditative experience but also reinforces positive associations with healing and empowerment.

Integrating these meditation techniques into your somatic therapy practice allows you to deepen your awareness and facilitate healing on multiple levels. As you embark on this journey, remember that there is no right or wrong way to meditate. The key is to find what feels most supportive and resonant for you. Whether through guided sessions, body scans, or vivid visualizations, you are creating a nurturing environment where your body and mind can work in harmony, paving the way for profound transformation and recovery. Embrace these practices as integral parts of your healing toolkit, and allow them to enrich your experience as you reclaim your body and restore your life.

Bringing Awareness to Your Daily Activities

Mindfulness can weave its way into the fabric of our everyday lives, transforming even the most mundane moments into powerful opportunities for healing and self-discovery. Imagine sitting down for a meal, perhaps a simple bowl of oatmeal or a vibrant salad. Instead of rushing through it while distracted by the television or your phone, take a moment to pause. Notice the colors, textures, and aromas of your food. As you take your first bite, slow down and really engage with the experience. Feel the warmth of the bowl in your hands, the subtle flavors on your tongue, and the satisfying sensation of nourishment filling your body. As thoughts drift in—worries about the day ahead or reflections on what's been—acknowledge them without judgment, allowing them to float away like leaves on a stream. This practice of mindful eating can transform meals into sacred moments of connection with yourself and your body.

Walking, too, offers a beautiful canvas for mindfulness. Next time you step outside, try to shift your focus from the destination to the journey itself. Feel your feet connecting with the ground beneath you, each step a gentle reminder of your presence in the world. Pay attention to the rhythm of your breath—notice how it syncs with your movement. Allow your senses to come alive; the rustle of leaves, the chirping of birds, the feel of the breeze against your skin. If your mind begins to wander to the stresses of daily life, gently bring it back to the sensations of walking, the experience of being fully alive in that moment. Walking mindfully can be a delightful practice that grounds you, helping to release tension and clear your mind.

Engaging in conversations can also become an opportunity for mindfulness. In our fast-paced world, it's easy to get caught up in the rush of exchanging ideas, often thinking about what we want to say next instead of truly listening. During your next conversation, try to approach it with a mindful heart. Notice the sound of the other person's voice, the expressions on their face, and the emotions conveyed in their words. Take a moment to pause before responding, allowing yourself to absorb what they're saying fully. As you speak, be aware of the sensations in your body—are you feeling relaxed or tense? Are your words flowing freely, or do you feel the weight of your thoughts? This practice not only enriches your interactions but also deepens your connection with others, fostering empathy and understanding.

You might even find mindfulness in your daily chores. Whether it's washing dishes, folding laundry, or taking out the trash, each task can be infused with presence. Feel the warm water as you scrub a plate, notice the smell of the soap, or the texture of the fabric as you fold. With each movement, bring your awareness to the sensations in your hands and arms, allowing the rhythm of the task to soothe your mind. In doing so, you transform chores into moments of tranquility, a practice of gratitude for the simple act of caring for your space.

By incorporating these mindful moments into your daily routine, you create a sanctuary of awareness that nurtures healing and resilience. Each experience becomes an invitation to explore your thoughts and emotions, helping you cultivate a deeper connection with yourself and the world around you. As you embrace mindfulness in these various activities, remember that it's not about achieving perfection; it's about showing up for yourself, one moment at a time.

Practicing Gratitude as a Somatic Tool

Gratitude plays a profound role in somatic healing and overall well-being, serving as a powerful antidote to the stresses and traumas we carry in our bodies. When we cultivate gratitude, we shift our focus from what we lack or the burdens we bear to the abundance of experiences and relationships that enrich our lives. This shift is not just a mental exercise; it has real physiological effects. Engaging in gratitude can reduce stress hormones, enhance mood, and even improve physical health by promoting relaxation and reducing muscle tension. In essence, gratitude helps to rewire our brains, allowing us to create a more positive narrative about our lives and experiences, which is essential for healing.

To encourage this transformative practice, consider incorporating specific exercises that help you reflect on and express gratitude in meaningful ways. One exercise is to create a daily gratitude ritual. Each morning or evening, take a few moments to sit quietly, breathe deeply, and reflect on three things you are grateful for. These can be simple pleasures, such as the warmth of the sun on your skin, a supportive friend, or even a delicious meal you enjoyed. As you think of each item, allow yourself to truly feel the emotion associated with your gratitude. Visualize how these positive experiences impact your life and your body, helping to cultivate a sense of safety and joy.

Another enriching practice involves journaling. Grab a notebook and set aside a few minutes each day to write about your gratitude. Instead of merely listing things, delve into why you are grateful for them. For example, if you are thankful for a friend, reflect on how their presence supports you, how their laughter brightens your day, and how they help you feel connected. This exercise encourages you not only to recognize the good in your life but also to explore the deeper emotional ties that contribute to your overall well-being. Over time, you may find that these reflections deepen your appreciation for your life and enhance your resilience against challenges.

You might also consider sharing your gratitude with others, which can foster connection and strengthen relationships. Try writing a heartfelt letter or note to someone who has made a positive impact on your life. Express specific ways in which they have supported you, encouraged you, or simply made you smile. Not only does this practice uplift the recipient, but it also reinforces your feelings of gratitude and connection. If you're feeling brave, you can even share your gratitude aloud during a gathering or meeting, creating a ripple effect of positivity that can uplift the whole group.

As you engage in these gratitude exercises, pay attention to how they make you feel physically. Notice if you experience a sense of warmth, openness, or lightness in your body. This connection between emotional and physical states highlights the holistic nature of healing—when we nurture our emotional well-being through gratitude, we also support our somatic health. So, embrace these practices, allow yourself to feel and express gratitude deeply, and witness how this shift in perspective can bolster your resilience, transforming your healing journey into one filled with light and hope.

Chapter 11

Healing Through Community and Connection

Group support can be a transformative aspect of the trauma recovery journey, providing a unique space where individuals can share their experiences and feelings in a safe environment. When people come together in a group setting, something magical happens: the barriers of isolation begin to dissolve. Many trauma survivors often feel alone in their struggles, burdened by the weight of their experiences. Yet, when they find themselves in a circle of peers who have walked similar paths, a sense of belonging emerges. This shared understanding fosters deep connections, reminding each participant that they are not alone in their pain.

Imagine a circle of individuals sitting together, each one carrying their own stories of trauma. As they take turns sharing, they discover that while their experiences may differ, the emotions attached to those experiences resonate deeply with one another. One person might share how they felt trapped in a cycle of anxiety following a traumatic event, while another might recount the overwhelming grief that came after a loss. As they listen and reflect, they realize they share a common thread—an unspoken understanding of fear, sorrow, and the longing for healing. In this space, vulnerability becomes a source of strength. Participants encourage one another, offering insights and support that come from a place of empathy. This dynamic fosters an atmosphere of acceptance, where everyone feels seen and heard.

Testimonials from individuals who have participated in group therapy highlight the profound impact of these shared experiences. One participant shared, "Before I joined the group, I felt like I was in a dark tunnel with no way out. But being with others who understood my pain made me feel like I could finally breathe again. It was like I found a light at the end of the tunnel, surrounded by people who truly got it." This sentiment captures the essence of group support—creating a safe haven where individuals can explore their vulnerabilities without judgment.

Additionally, group settings can provide an opportunity for individuals to witness others' journeys toward healing. When participants share their progress, no matter how small, it serves as a beacon of hope for others in the group. Hearing stories of resilience can spark motivation and inspire those who may still feel stuck in their trauma. One woman recounted how she attended group sessions for several months before she began to feel a shift in her mindset. "I watched others start to reclaim their lives, and it pushed me to try things I never thought I could do. I learned that healing isn't linear, and that was okay." Such insights highlight how the collective strength of a group can encourage personal breakthroughs and foster a sense of hope that feels tangible.

Moreover, engaging in group support can also teach essential social skills that may have been hindered by trauma. Many survivors struggle with trust and communication, finding it challenging to open up or engage with others. Within the group, participants practice these skills in a nurturing environment, gradually rebuilding their confidence in connecting with others. A participant noted, "At first, I was terrified to speak up. But as I listened to others and shared my own story, I felt a shift. I began to understand that I wasn't alone in feeling vulnerable. It helped me find my voice again." This reclamation of voice is a crucial step in the healing process, enabling individuals to express their feelings and needs in a way that feels safe and supported.

The impact of group dynamics can be particularly profound in trauma recovery. Participants often develop a sense of accountability to one another, which can motivate them to engage more actively in their healing process. As they build connections and friendships, they often find themselves looking forward to each session, knowing they are not just attending a meeting, but joining a community. In many cases, group members form bonds that extend beyond the therapy setting, supporting one another in their everyday lives, creating a network of encouragement and friendship that can be incredibly healing.

These shared experiences in group support not only enhance individual healing but also cultivate a collective resilience. When participants witness the strength and courage of their peers, they begin to recognize their own potential for healing. Through the journey of sharing, listening, and supporting one another, they create a powerful community that stands together, fostering connection and hope in the face of adversity. This sense of camaraderie can be an invaluable resource, reinforcing the idea that while the journey of trauma recovery is deeply personal, it doesn't have to be traveled alone.

Creating Your Own Support System

Building a personal support system is a crucial step on your journey to healing, and it can be both empowering and reassuring to know that you don't have to navigate this path alone. Surrounding yourself with friends, family, and professionals who genuinely understand

and validate your experiences can significantly impact your recovery from trauma. Start by reflecting on the relationships you already have. Identify those individuals who offer kindness, empathy, and support, as these are the people who can provide a safe space for you to express your feelings and experiences.

When it comes to communicating your needs, honesty is key. You might feel hesitant to share your struggles with those close to you, fearing they may not understand or might feel uncomfortable. However, approaching these conversations with vulnerability can foster deeper connections. Begin by expressing what you're going through in a way that feels comfortable for you. For instance, you might say, "I've been dealing with some challenging feelings lately, and I could really use your support." This simple statement opens the door for dialogue, inviting your loved ones to step into your world and offer their understanding.

Setting boundaries is another essential aspect of building a supportive network. It's perfectly okay to let people know what you need in terms of space and interaction. If you're feeling overwhelmed, communicate that you may need some quiet time or that you prefer to keep certain topics off the table for now. Clear boundaries not only protect your well-being but also help others understand how to best support you. Remember, boundaries are not walls; they are simply guidelines that help you maintain your emotional safety.

Seeking out supportive relationships also means being intentional about who you spend your time with. Surround yourself with individuals who not only listen but also validate your feelings. These people can be friends, family members, or even support group members who share similar experiences. Look for communities—whether online or in-person—that resonate with your journey. Connecting with others who have faced trauma can create a sense of camaraderie, reminding you that you're not alone and that your feelings are both valid and shared.

Additionally, don't hesitate to seek professional support if you feel it would benefit you. A therapist or counselor can provide a specialized form of understanding and guidance that friends and family may not be equipped to offer. When choosing a professional, consider what qualities are important to you—whether it's someone who is empathetic, has experience in trauma recovery, or uses somatic approaches. The right professional can help you navigate your feelings and experiences, providing strategies that align with your unique needs.

As you build your support system, keep in mind that it's a dynamic process. Relationships will evolve, and that's perfectly normal. You may find that some connections strengthen while others fade away. That's okay. The goal is to create a network of people who uplift and empower you, those who understand your journey and encourage you to embrace your healing process. Celebrate the small victories along the way and recognize that every step you take toward building this support system is a step toward reclaiming your life and your well-being. Surrounding yourself with understanding, validating people is a gift you give yourself—a reminder that healing is a journey best taken with others by your side.

Working with a Somatic Therapist: What to Expect

Working with a somatic therapist can be a deeply transformative experience, offering a pathway to healing that acknowledges the profound connection between mind and body. When you first step into a somatic therapy session, the journey typically begins with an initial assessment. This is a time for you and the therapist to get to know each other, establishing a safe space where you can share your experiences and concerns. The therapist will ask you about your history, focusing not only on past traumas but also on your current physical sensations and emotional states. This conversation is not just about your mental health; it's an invitation to tune into your body, exploring how your physical experiences might be linked to your emotional landscape.

As you delve deeper into your personal narrative, the therapist will work with you to set specific goals for your therapy. These goals might range from reducing anxiety and stress to developing greater body awareness or finding strategies to cope with emotional triggers. It's essential to approach this process collaboratively, ensuring that your voice is central to the therapeutic journey. Together, you'll create a roadmap for your healing, a guide that aligns with your unique needs and aspirations.

Somatic therapy is rich with a variety of techniques designed to engage the body and facilitate healing. These may include breathwork, where you'll learn to harness the power of your breath to calm the nervous system and ground yourself in the present moment. Gentle movement practices, such as somatic yoga or stretching, help release tension stored in the muscles and promote a sense of freedom in your body. The therapist may also introduce guided visualizations or mindfulness exercises that encourage you to connect with and explore your physical sensations in a non-judgmental way. These techniques create an opportunity for you to process emotions and experiences stored in your body, fostering a deeper understanding of yourself.

When seeking a somatic therapist, it's important to look for certain qualities that can significantly enhance your healing journey. A good somatic therapist should possess a deep understanding of trauma and how it affects both the mind and body. They should exude compassion and empathy, creating a safe space where you feel comfortable exploring difficult emotions and experiences. Additionally, they should be skilled in a variety of somatic techniques, allowing for flexibility in addressing your unique needs. It's also beneficial to find someone who encourages open communication, inviting you to share your thoughts and feelings about the therapeutic process as it unfolds.

Preparing for your somatic therapy sessions can also enhance the effectiveness of your experience. Before a session, it's helpful to take a few moments to reflect on what you want to focus on during your time together. Consider keeping a journal to jot down any physical sensations, emotions, or experiences that come to mind in the days leading up to your appointment. This can provide valuable insights for your therapist and help you articulate your needs more clearly. On the day of the session, try to arrive a bit early to allow yourself to transition into the space calmly. Wearing comfortable clothing can also facilitate movement and relaxation during the session, making it easier for you to connect with your body without restrictions.

By approaching somatic therapy with openness and curiosity, you can embark on a healing journey that embraces the wisdom of your body. With the guidance of a skilled therapist, this process can lead to profound insights and transformations, allowing you to reclaim your sense of safety and well-being in your own skin.

Finding Somatic Support Groups and Resources

When it comes to finding somatic support groups, online communities, and additional resources for trauma recovery, there's a wealth of options available that can make your journey feel less lonely and more empowered. One of the most effective ways to connect with others who share similar experiences is through organizations that specialize in somatic therapy and trauma recovery. For instance, the **Somatic Experiencing Trauma Institute** offers workshops, training programs, and a directory of practitioners across the globe. Their website provides a treasure trove of resources, including articles and community forums where you can engage with others on the same path.

Another fantastic place to explore is **The Trauma Research Foundation**, which not only conducts cutting-edge research on trauma but also hosts events and workshops aimed at connecting individuals with supportive practices. Their resources can help you find local support groups, training opportunities, and a community of people focused on healing. Similarly, organizations like **The Center for Nonviolent Communication** foster connection and understanding, offering workshops and community groups that emphasize empathetic communication—a vital component of the healing process.

For those who prefer the digital landscape, there are numerous online communities where you can share experiences and find encouragement. Websites like **Reddit** have dedicated forums, such as r/trauma and r/mentalhealth, where you can interact with others, share your story, and gain insight from diverse perspectives. Facebook groups are another excellent avenue; searching for "somatic therapy" or "trauma recovery" will lead you to vibrant communities where members support one another with resources, advice, and a sense of belonging.

If you're looking for additional materials to deepen your understanding, consider checking out the **National Institute for the Clinical Application of Behavioral Medicine (NICABM)**, which offers webinars and courses focused on trauma-informed care and somatic techniques. Their content is often enriched by the insights of experienced practitioners who can provide guidance on integrating these practices into your daily life.

For more localized support, consider reaching out to mental health clinics or wellness centers in your area that offer somatic therapy or trauma-informed practices. Many of these centers host support groups where you can meet others in a safe, nurturing environment. Local universities or community colleges might also have programs or workshops on somatic therapy or trauma recovery, so don't hesitate to explore these avenues.

Lastly, keep in mind that healing is not a solitary endeavor. Seeking out supportive environments is crucial, and there's no shortage of resources waiting to guide you. The connections you make, whether in person or online, can be a powerful reminder that you are not alone on this journey. Engaging with communities and individuals who understand your

experiences can foster healing and help you reclaim a
sense of safety and empowerment in your life.

"

Chapter 12

Your Ongoing Journey – Life After Trauma Recovery

What Does Life After Trauma Recovery Look Like?

Life after trauma recovery can be a vibrant tapestry woven with threads of growth, joy, and resilience. Imagine waking up each morning with a sense of possibility, where the sun filtering through your window feels like a gentle reminder that today is a new opportunity. The heaviness that once accompanied your thoughts begins to lift, replaced by a lightness that invites exploration and connection. You may find yourself laughing more easily, savoring the taste of your favorite meals, or relishing the warmth of friendships that have deepened as you embraced your journey toward healing.

As you move through life, the skills you've developed through somatic practices become your allies. You might recall how, in moments of stress or anxiety, you learned to pause and tune in to your body. This newfound awareness helps you recognize the physical sensations that signal discomfort or unease, allowing you to respond with kindness rather than fear. When triggers arise—perhaps during a conversation that unexpectedly echoes the past—you have the tools to ground yourself. Breathing deeply, feeling your feet on the ground, and returning to the present moment become instinctual. With each practice, you reclaim more of your space, and the world around you feels a little less overwhelming.

Yet, it's important to acknowledge that the path to recovery is not always smooth. Common challenges can arise as you navigate your new life. You might encounter moments of doubt or fear, questioning whether you've truly moved past your trauma. There may be days when old memories resurface, and you find yourself wrestling with emotions you thought you had put behind you. This is a natural part of the healing process, and it's crucial to remember that growth isn't linear.

In these moments, lean into the resilience you've cultivated. The somatic practices you've embraced—mindful breathing, gentle movement, and grounding techniques—can help you regain your footing. Instead of viewing these challenges as setbacks, see them as opportunities for deeper understanding. Each time you face a difficult moment, you're not just surviving; you're learning more about yourself and the strengths you possess.

Visualize a future where you embrace your vulnerability as a source of strength. Imagine engaging in relationships that nourish your soul, where you feel safe to share your thoughts and emotions without fear of judgment. Picture yourself pursuing passions that ignite your spirit, whether it's picking up a long-lost hobby, volunteering for a cause close to your heart, or simply spending more time in nature. These moments of joy can become the cornerstones of your new life, paving the way for a fulfilling existence rooted in authenticity.

As you navigate the complexities of life after trauma, remember that you're not alone on this journey. Surround yourself with a supportive community—friends, family, or even fellow survivors—who can encourage you and share in your triumphs. Their presence can be a powerful reminder that healing is a collective experience, where shared stories and mutual understanding foster a sense of belonging.

Life after trauma recovery is not just about returning to who you were; it's about evolving into someone stronger, wiser, and more attuned to your own needs. You have the power to visualize a future filled with possibility—a life that is not defined by your past but enriched by your experiences. Embrace this potential, and trust in your ability to navigate whatever challenges may come your way.

Staying Grounded in Your Progress

Maintaining a sense of grounding and connection to the progress you've made in your recovery journey is essential for sustaining long-term well-being. One powerful way to do this is by celebrating small victories. Each step you take, no matter how minor it may seem, is a testament to your resilience and commitment to healing. Perhaps you managed to stay present during a challenging moment or tried a new somatic practice that resonated with you. These small wins deserve acknowledgment because they collectively contribute to your growth. Consider keeping a victory journal where you jot down these moments. This practice not only highlights your achievements but also provides a tangible reminder of your journey when you revisit it.

Reflecting on your growth is another important strategy for maintaining connection to your recovery. Regularly take time to pause and look back on where you started and how far you've come. This reflection can be as simple as a quiet moment in nature or a more structured practice, like writing a letter to your past self. In this letter, you can express compassion for the struggles you faced and acknowledge the strength it took to overcome them. By framing your experiences in this way, you cultivate a deeper understanding of your journey and the resilience that has emerged from it.

Integrating somatic practices into your daily routine is crucial for sustaining the well-being you've worked hard to achieve. Incorporate mindful breathing or gentle movement into your morning or evening rituals. These practices not only ground you in the present but also reinforce the connection between your mind and body, helping to release any accumulated tension. For instance, you might start your day with a few minutes of deep breathing, focusing on the sensation of your breath filling your lungs. As you inhale, imagine drawing in calmness, and as you exhale, visualize releasing any stress or worries. This simple yet powerful practice can set a positive tone for your day.

Another effective exercise is to engage in mindful walking, where each step is an opportunity to connect with your body and the earth beneath your feet. As you walk, pay attention to the sensation of your feet making contact with the ground and the rhythm of your breath. This practice not only helps ground you but also creates a moving meditation that can soothe anxious thoughts and reconnect you with the present moment.

Additionally, finding a supportive community or engaging in group practices can enhance your sense of connection and accountability. Sharing your experiences and listening to others can be incredibly validating, reminding you that you're not alone on this journey. Whether it's a support group or a class focused on somatic therapy, surrounding yourself with like-minded individuals fosters an environment of encouragement and shared growth.

Throughout your journey, remember to be gentle with yourself. Healing is not linear, and there will be ups and downs. By consistently celebrating your progress, reflecting on your growth, and integrating somatic practices into your daily life, you create a nurturing framework that supports your ongoing recovery. Each moment spent grounding yourself in these practices is an affirmation of your strength and commitment to living a fulfilling, empowered life.

Setting New Goals for Growth and Healing

As you continue on your journey of recovery, it's important to embrace the power of goal-setting. Setting new, meaningful goals not only gives you a sense of direction but also helps you celebrate how far you've come. Take a moment to reflect on your past achievements—no matter how small they may seem. Maybe you've learned to identify a trigger before it overwhelms you, or perhaps you've incorporated mindfulness practices into your daily routine. Acknowledging these milestones is essential; they remind you that progress is real and tangible. Each step forward, no matter its size, is a testament to your resilience and commitment to healing.

Once you've celebrated those achievements, turn your gaze to the future. What areas in your life do you feel are ripe for further growth? It could be enhancing your somatic practices, deepening your connections with others, or exploring new interests that excite you. This reflective process isn't about putting pressure on yourself to achieve perfection; it's about nurturing a sense of curiosity and openness toward what you want to cultivate in your life. Consider writing down these areas for growth, allowing yourself to articulate what feels important to you right now.

Incorporating somatic practices into your new goals can create a beautiful synergy between your body and mind. Think about how you can weave movement, breathwork, or mindfulness into your everyday activities. For instance, you might set a goal to practice a specific somatic exercise a few times a week or commit to a daily breathing ritual. These practices can serve as both a grounding mechanism and a source of empowerment, enabling you to connect deeply with your body while moving forward.

As you embark on this goal-setting process, remember the importance of adaptability. Life is unpredictable, and your healing journey may take unexpected turns. Being flexible in your goals allows you to adjust them as needed, respecting your evolving needs and circumstances. If a particular somatic practice doesn't resonate with you as it once did, it's perfectly okay to explore new avenues. Embracing adaptability means recognizing that your journey is uniquely yours, and it's okay to change direction or take a step back when needed. Allow yourself the grace to adapt and evolve as you navigate this path toward healing and empowerment.

Ultimately, setting meaningful goals is about aligning your intentions with your lived experience, honoring both your past and the possibilities that lie ahead. Each new goal you set can become a beacon of hope and a reminder that healing is not only possible but also a journey of continuous growth and discovery.

Continuing Your Journey with Compassion

In the intricate landscape of healing from trauma, one of the most vital tools you can cultivate is self-compassion. This gentle practice allows you to approach your healing journey with kindness and understanding, especially during those inevitable moments of difficulty or setback. It's all too easy to fall into the trap of self-criticism when you encounter challenges, feeling like you're not progressing fast enough or that you should be "over it" by now. However, embracing self-compassion means recognizing that healing is not a linear process. There will be ups and downs, and that's perfectly okay.

To nurture this self-kindness, start by simply acknowledging your feelings without judgment. When you find yourself struggling, take a moment to pause and breathe. Instead of pushing those feelings away or berating yourself for having them, gently remind yourself that it's human to experience pain and setbacks. It's part of the journey. You might say to yourself, "I'm going through a tough time, and that's understandable. I deserve patience and kindness right now." This small shift in perspective can create a safe space for healing, allowing you to face your emotions with warmth rather than resistance.

One effective way to practice self-compassion is through affirmations. These simple yet powerful statements can serve as daily reminders of your worth and resilience. Consider repeating phrases like, "I am enough, just as I am," or "It's okay to take my time in healing." Each time you affirm these truths, you reinforce a compassionate mindset, gradually replacing self-doubt with self-love. You might also want to keep a journal where you jot down your feelings and reflections. On difficult days, write a letter to yourself as if you were speaking to a dear friend who is struggling. What would you say to them? By treating yourself with the same care and concern, you can learn to nurture that same kindness within.

Reflective exercises can also help in cultivating self-compassion. One such exercise involves visualizing a comforting figure—this could be a loved one, a mentor, or even a fictional character—who embodies kindness and support. Imagine this figure standing by your side, offering words of encouragement and compassion. What would they say to you during challenging moments? How would they help you navigate your feelings? Allow this visualization to envelop you in warmth and support, reminding you that you are never alone in your struggles.

As you continue on your healing journey, remember that setbacks do not erase the progress you've made. They are simply part of the ebb and flow of recovery. Practicing self-compassion helps you build resilience, allowing you to bounce back and keep moving forward. Embrace each moment, even the difficult ones, with a sense of curiosity and compassion. When you can meet yourself with kindness, you create a nurturing environment where true healing can take place.

Conclusion

Your Path to a Peaceful, Empowered Life

As you embark on this journey of healing, it's important to remember that recovery is not a destination but a continuous process. Each step you take is part of a larger path toward reclaiming your life and well-being. Trauma can leave deep scars, but it doesn't define you. Embracing the journey means accepting that there will be ups and downs, moments of clarity and moments of struggle. This ebb and flow is perfectly normal, and acknowledging it allows you to be more compassionate with yourself.

Throughout this process, you've gathered tools to help you navigate the complexities of stress, anxiety, and emotional flashbacks. Whether it's through mindful breathing, grounding techniques, or gentle movement, you have empowered yourself with strategies that can ease the weight of trauma. These tools aren't just temporary fixes; they are skills you can revisit and refine as you move forward. Think of them as your personal toolkit, ready to support you whenever challenges arise.

Somatic therapy, in particular, offers a unique way to stay connected to your body and emotions, facilitating a deeper understanding of your experiences. As you continue to practice somatic techniques, you'll find that they can enhance your emotional resilience and physical well-being. The beauty of somatic therapy lies in its adaptability; you can integrate these practices into your daily life in ways that resonate with you. Perhaps it's a few minutes of mindful breathing before starting your day, or a gentle movement session to release tension after a stressful event. Whatever form it takes, the act of tuning into your body will remain a powerful ally in your healing journey.

Remember that growth often happens in small, subtle ways. You might notice an increased sense of calm in situations that once felt overwhelming or an ability to recognize your triggers without being swept away by them. Each of these victories, no matter how small, is a testament to your progress and commitment to healing. Celebrate these moments, as they contribute to your overall growth and resilience.

As you move forward, let the knowledge that you're not alone be a source of comfort. Many others share this path, and their stories can inspire and uplift you. Engage with communities, whether in person or online, where you can share experiences, challenges, and victories. Connection with others can provide invaluable support and encouragement, reminding you that healing is a shared human experience.

In this journey, be gentle with yourself. Allow yourself the grace to stumble, to feel, and to grow. Your commitment to healing is a courageous step toward living a more fulfilling, empowered life. Embrace this ongoing journey, knowing that every effort you make enriches not only your life but also the lives of those around you. Through somatic therapy and your newfound practices, you are laying the foundation for a future where emotional and physical well-being is not just a goal, but a vibrant reality.